175 Fresh Card Ideas

Designs to make and give throughout the year

By Kimber McGray

NORTH LIGHT BOOKS
CINCINNATI, OHIO

175 Fresh Card Ideas. Copyright © 2010 by Kimber McGray. Manufactured in China. All rights reserved. No part of this book may be reproduced in any form or by any electronic or mechanical means including information storage and retrieval systems without permission in writing from the publisher, except by a reviewer who may quote brief passages in a review. Published by North Light Books, an imprint of F+W Media, Inc., 4700 East Galbraith Road, Cincinnati, Ohio, 45236. (800) 289-0963. First Edition.

www.fwmedia.com

14 13 12 11 10   5 4 3 2 1

DISTRIBUTED IN CANADA BY FRASER DIRECT
100 Armstrong Avenue
Georgetown, ON, Canada L7G 5S4
Tel: (905) 877-4411

DISTRIBUTED IN THE U.K. AND EUROPE BY DAVID & CHARLES
Brunel House, Newton Abbot, Devon, TQ12 4PU, England
Tel: (+44) 1626 323200, Fax: (+44) 1626 323319
Email: postmaster@davidandcharles.co.uk

DISTRIBUTED IN AUSTRALIA BY CAPRICORN LINK
P.O. Box 704, S. Windsor NSW, 2756 Australia
Tel: (02) 4577-3555

Library of Congress Cataloging in Publication Data
McGray, Kimber.
  175 fresh card ideas : designs to make and give throughout the year / by Kimber McGray. – 1st ed.
    p. cm.
  Includes index.
  ISBN 978-1-4403-0792-8 (pbk. : alk. paper)
  1. Greeting cards. I. Title. II. Title: One hundred and fifty plus fresh card ideas.
  TT872.M35 2010
  745.594'1–dc22
                                      2010001950

Edited by Julie Hollyday
Designed by Corrie Schaffeld
Production coordinated by Greg Nock
Photography by Christine Polomsky, Al Parrish
Card sketch illustration by Paula Gilarde

Metric Conversion Chart

To convert	to	multiply by
Inches	Centimeters	2.54
Centimeters	Inches	0.4
Feet	Centimeters	30.5
Centimeters	Feet	0.03
Yards	Meters	0.9
Meters	Yards	1.1

Dedication

This book is dedicated to Lily Jackson and Jordan Pruis. I am thrilled to see two talented young ladies enjoy card making as much as they do.

Acknowledgments

In the current world with electronic communication, the way that we connect with our friends and family the most, it is still so delightful when we receive a handmade card in our mailbox from a friend or loved one to show they are thinking of us. This became clearer to me while my husband was deployed to Iraq for a year. A group of wonderful card makers sent over boxes of handmade cards for the soldiers to send back to their families and friends. While I got to e-mail with my husband on a fairly regular basis, it was such a nice surprise to have cards in my mailbox for both me and my children to show he was thinking of us. There is just something about "real mail" that made us smile that much brighter.

All the cards featured in this book will be donated to the group that is instrumental in supplying my husband's group of soldiers and many others that are stationed around the world serving our country, Operation Write Home (operationwritehome.org).

I want to thank the members of Operation Write Home from the bottom of my heart for supporting the troops and, by doing so, my family. Your hard work is truly inspiring.

I would also like to thank my family and friends that supported me again while working on this project. Their patience and understanding make doing these projects more enjoyable.

To the fantastic contributors, your cards were truly inspiring to me as I worked on projects for the book. Thank you for creating the wonderful cards and then donating them to Operation Write Home.

A special thank you to Paula Gilarde who assisted in turning my hand drawn sketches into digital images featured on pages 122-123.

Also, thanks goes to my acquisitions editor, Kristin Boys, and editor, Julie Hollyday, who were instrumental from the beginning in getting this project off the ground quickly and believing in me.

About the Author

Kimber McGray is a 2007 Creative Keepsakes Hall of Fame winner who teaches at her local scrapbook store and guest teaches at other locations across the United States and Canada, including at a Creating Keepsakes Convention and the Canada's Scrapbooking Crop for the Kids. She currently works on the design teams for the following manufacturers and regularly attends CHA with them: We R Memory Keepers, Core'dinations, Jillibean Soup and Unity Stamp Company. Kimber is the co-author of *Remember This*, the author of *Scrapbook Secrets* and has contributed artwork to numerous other books and magazines.

Table of Contents

Introduction

We live in a fast-paced world, full of commotion and obligations that vie for our time. When you have friends and family all over the country and the world, keeping in touch usually means a quick e-mail or a lengthy telephone conversation. These are convenient ways to stay connected to the ones you love.

But think about seeing your name handwritten on an envelope that contains a simple card. This card might make you laugh, it might make you cry, but it will certainly make you feel special.

There is nothing better than getting a handmade card in the mail. Making and sending cards can be just as quick and easy as sending an e-mail, and can say as much as a lengthy phone conversation.

My children love to make cards to send to their grandparents. We cherished receiving cards from my husband while he was deployed in Iraq. The unexpected note from a friend that simply says she is thinking about you makes your day brighter. These are the reasons we make and send cards. Of course, we crafters enjoy the process of creating the card but, I can tell you, the recipient will enjoy it even more.

In this book, I gathered some of the best card makers out there to give you new ideas to put to use in your card making. Use the simple techniques to build beautiful cards that can say anything from "Happy Birthday" to "Happy Holidays" to "Just thinking about you."

As a bonus, you'll get ideas for presenting gifts that accompany your cards, and galleries full of inspiration.

As easy as sending an e-mail, make a card today, and let someone know they're special.

Card Maker's Toolbox

Compared to the amount of materials necessary to some crafts, the supplies you need to make beautiful cards are relatively few. But within this basic list, including paper, punches and embellishments, your options are almost unlimited. Add your fabulous imagination, and you'll be making beautiful handmade cards in no time!

Papers

Paper can bring a lot to a design, whether it be whimsy, beauty or even structure. There are two types of paper you'll need to made cards.

Heavyweight cardstock is the base of your card design. The heavier weight cardstocks will hold up better to mailing and general handling than thinner weight paper like designer paper or patterned paper. Cardstock between 60lbs and 80lbs will fold nicely and provide a strong base for your designs; anything heavier will be difficult to fold cleanly.

Patterned papers can give your card its personality. There are so many different designs and styles out there. It can be a bit overwhelming at times. Just go with what you like and what fits the style of the cards you create. You can't go wrong.

Stamps and Inks

Stamps add a variety of figures, flourishes and words to your cards. The inks you choose will depend on the colors and look you want.

Rubber stamps are the most durable type of stamps and tend to produce the cleanest and sharpest images. Rubber stamps can come either premounted on a woodblock or unmounted, with or without a layer of foam. The foam is an important component of a clean-stamped image. If you purchase unmounted rubber stamps, you can buy foam to layer between the rubber stamp piece and the mounting block.

Clear stamps have benefits and challenges. It's much easier to see where you are placing your stamp image since you can see through the stamp. Clear stamps aren't as durable as rubber stamps, and need to be stored properly for the longest usage life. Store them on a smooth, nonporous surface to keep them clean. If they don't stick to the mounting block, you can wash them with mild soap and warm water and let them air dry.

All stamps should be stored out of direct heat and direct sunlight, as these elements can deteriorate the stamps faster.

When it comes to inks for the stamps, you can find many

types of inks and a wide variety of colors. Here are some of the most basic categories.

Dye ink dries quickly and can absorb into the paper, depending on the brand. These inks come in a variety of colors. Read the labels carefully to find out if the ink you choose is waterproof or not.

Pigment ink provides a more vibrant image. Because the ink sits on the surface of the paper, it dries more slowly, making it ideal for heat embossing. Heat setting will help the ink to dry more quickly.

Chalk ink gives a softer, more blurred image. It is best used for coloring the edges of paper because it gives a soft, blended effect.

See page 17 for a neat technique that uses ink to add depth to card borders.

Embellishments

The key to embellishing cards is to keep the items you add light; heavy embellishments can bend the paper and create unwanted creases. The following embellishments can add a ton of visual, sometimes even dimensional punch without weighing the card down.

Ribbons and trims offer endless choices. While you can find many varieties in paper stores, check out your local fabric stores as well. Silk and grosgrain ribbons create beautiful bows, while twills and twines are great for masculine cards.

Buttons are a nice flat embellishment to add to your card for a finishing touch. You can find buttons almost everywhere; paper stores and fabric stores carry

nice selections. You can even salvage buttons from old clothing.

Chipboard pieces come in all shapes and sizes. They offer quick solutions for card makers who want to add extra dimension to their cards, and are easy to decorate to match card designs. You can also find predecorated chipboard shapes; look around and see if they inspire a card design.

Embossed embellishments can add delicious texture to card designs. Dry embossing leaves an imprint on the paper, and it can be created a few different ways. A simple way is to use brass stencils and a stylus. Another option is to use one of the many new machines and tools on the market; these machines make it almost foolproof and offer a wide variety of designs. Check out page 15 for basic instructions for using one of these machines.

Heat embossing creates a smooth, raised image. You need a few items to add heat embossing to a card. You'll need a stamp of your choosing; a pigment ink or an embossing ink, and embossing powder. A heat gun is used to melt the embossing powder into the smooth, raised image. See page 14 for how to execute this technique.

There are even more possibilities for embellishments. **Pens and markers** can help add details and colors. Copic Markers are increasingly being found in card makers' toolboxes because they produce beautiful colors and shading, and they have a high archival quality. A **basic sewing machine** can do double duty of securing elements to and decorating your cards with straight and zigzag stitches. If you don't have a basic sewing machine you can hand

stitch with a **needle and thread** or faux stitch on your cards as a substitution (see page 12 for the techniques). The techniques and cards in this book will provide you with more than enough ideas.

Adhesives

Adhesives take your pretty designs and hold them together. You'll want a variety of adhesives on hand to tackle any design situation.

Dry adhesives, such as permanent tape runners, are for adhering decorative papers to the front of cards. **Wet adhesives**, including liquid glue and glue sticks, are also for adhering decorative papers to the front of cards, but you should use them sparingly because too much wet glue can cause the papers to curl.

Foam adhesive, often called "pop-up tape," allows you to add dimension to your designs. Foam adhesives come in a range of thicknesses to give your embellishments height.

Adhesive dots (like Glue Dots) are perfect for adhering small embellishments, such as buttons, to the card front.

Basic Tools

Basic punches and dies are some of the most used items in a card maker's toolbox. I recommend a corner rounder punch as well as a few sizes of circle and square punches.

Border punches create a shaped border, like scallops, that add a nice touch to card designs. Turn to page 13 to learn how to use a border punch as part of a design.

Scissors are a mainstay for any card maker. You will probably want a variety of scissors that can add details. I recommend having one pair of detail scissors for cutting into small areas of paper, and another pair of scissors dedicated to cutting ribbons and trims. Ribbon scissors should be used for only ribbons because paper would dull their blades, making it difficult to cut ribbon properly.

A **basic paper trimmer** that can cut a 12" × 12" (30.5cm × 30.5cm) or an 8½" × 11" (21.5cm × 28cm) piece of paper is a necessity. If you don't purchase premade card blanks, you will need to cut the paper down to the right size. Paper trimmers make these cuts more quickly and equally than handcutting.

A **craft knife** is nice to have in your toolbox to use for cutting when scissors prove to be too bulky. Keeping a few extra blades on hand is a good idea, because fresh blades make cutting easier.

A **scoring tool** can create a crease in the paper for a clean and crisp fold. Many paper trimmers come with scoring blades you can use in conjunction with your trimmers. You can also use a **bone folder** and a **ruler** to score papers. Before folding a piece of paper in half to create a card blank, use a scoring tool to create the crease, allowing for a clean fold line. This can help keep some cardstocks from cracking when folded. There are a few different methods to create the crease, but I show you my favorite method on page 11 using a Scor-Pal.

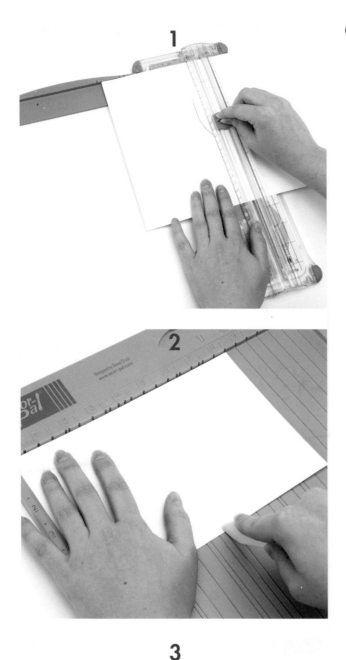

Techniques

As with every craft, there are always some great basics that can get you started on the right foot. After you've mastered the basics, tackle a fun, new technique and challenge yourself.

Making a Card Base

Creating a standard A2 sized, 5½" × 4¼" (14cm × 10.75cm), card blank from a piece of cardstock is simple as 1, 2, 3.

MATERIALS

Cardstock • Paper trimmer
Scoring tool (Scor-Pal) • Bone folder

1 If you have a piece of 8½" × 11" (21.5cm × 28cm) cardstock, cut it in half to 5½" × 8½" (14cm × 21.5cm). If you have a 12" × 12" (30.5cm × 30.5cm) piece of cardstock, cut it down to 8½" × 11" (21.5cm × 28cm), and then cut it in half to 5½" × 8½" (14cm × 21.5cm).

2 Place the 5½" × 8½" (14cm × 21.5cm) piece of cardstock onto the scoring tool and square the edges of the paper to the sides of the scoring tool. Using the pointed end of the bone folder, score the length of the cardstock at the 4¼" (10.75cm) mark.

3 Remove the cardstock from the scoring tool and fold the cardstock at the score. Using the side of the bone folder, crease the cardstock at the fold.

Faux Stitching
with a Pen

A quick and easy way to give a finishing "stitch" to your card is to use a pen. The card on page 33 uses this technique.

M A T E R I A L S

T-square or ruler • Pen

1 Using the ruler or the t-square, draw a straight dashed line with the pen.

2 Take your time going around curved edges and create the same length of stitches all around the border.

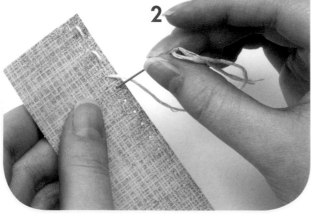

Hand Stitching

Adding embroidered stitching to a card creates a warm and homespun touch. This technique is used to embellish many cards throughout the book.

M A T E R I A L S

Paper • Stitching guide • Foam mat
Needle • Paper piercer • Thread or embroidery floss

1 Using the stitching guide, poke holes through the paper and into a foam mat with the paper piercer.

2 With an embroidery needle and thread, stitch along the punched lines.

1

Punches

Punches can add many different looks to a project. A border punch used in layers gives dimension to a handmade embellishment. This technique is put to good use with the card design on page 54.

MATERIALS

Border punch • Cardstock • Adhesive
Scissors

1 Line up the cardstock along the edge of the punch. Press the punch lever down to create the decorative edge.

2

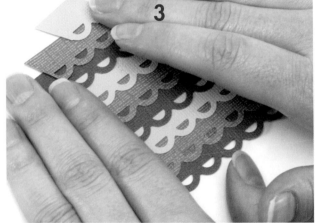

2 Slide the punched edge along the printed design and line it up with the pattern guide. Press the punched lever again to continue the decorative edge. Repeat to create all the edges you need.

3

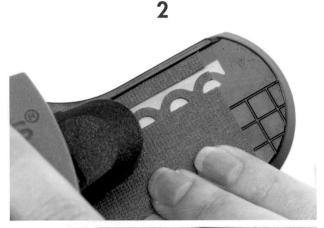

3 Layer and adhere the decorative edged papers.

4 Trim off the excess lengths to create the embellishment. I created a Christmas tree.

4

Heat Embossing

Heat embossing can add a stunning touch to your cards. Turn to page 67 to see the fantastic results using this technique.

M A T E R I A L S

Embossing ink or pigment ink • Stamp
Embossing powder • Heat gun

1 Using either an embossing ink or a pigment ink, stamp an image onto the paper.

2 Pour embossing powder over the stamped image to cover it completely. Shake off the excess powder.

3 Heat the embossing powder until the powder melts. Keep the heat gun moving so you don't scorch your paper.

1

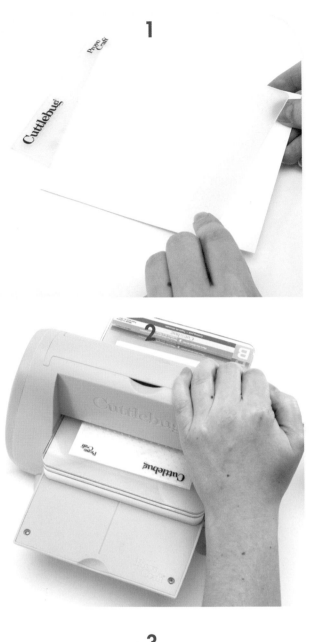

Dry Embossing

The quickest way to give your card a punch of texture is to dry emboss paper with a machine and an embossing folder. The card on page 84 makes good use of this technique.

MATERIALS

Embossing folder
Embossing machine (Provo Craft Cuttlebug)

1 Lay the cardstock in the embossing folder.

2 Run the embossing folder through the machine.

3 Remove the cardstock from the embossing folder.

3

Paper Piecing

A fun way to add some dimension with stamping is to create paper pieced images. See this technique in action on page 53.

M A T E R I A L S

Stamp • Ink • Cardstock, a variety

Foam adhesive

1 Stamp the same image on a few different pieces of cardstock.

2 Cut out each layer you want to piece.

3 Assemble the different layers, using the foam adhesive between each layer, to create a dimensional image.

Inking Edges

A light hand and the right ink can create a soft, distressed edge. Layering different papers that have inked edges adds great depth and interest to cards. The card design on page 109 shows this technique well.

MATERIALS

Chalk ink • Paper

1 Gently swipe the chalk ink pad over the edge of the card. If you angle it more toward the card, you will place more ink on the paper; angling it away from the card (more upright) will put less ink on the card.

2 Repeat on other papers and layer.

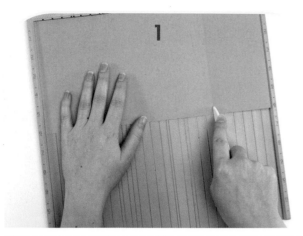

Gift Card Holder

This basic gift card holder design can be re-created for birthdays, Christmas, baby showers and so much more by simply changing the papers and embellishments you use. The card on page 87 features this impressive technique.

MATERIALS

Paper • Scoring tool (Scor-Pal) • Bone folder
Craft knife • Circle punch • Adhesive

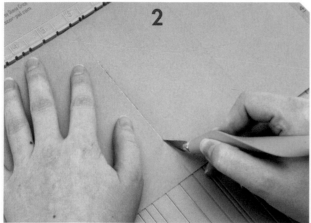

1 Using a 6" × 12" (15.25cm × 30.5cm) piece of paper, score at 3" (7.5cm), 6" (15.25cm) and 9" (22.75cm); this creates four panels.

2 Slice the paper at the 6" (15.25cm) score mark leaving at least 1" uncut (2.5cm) at both ends.

3 Place adhesive along the 3 sides of panel 2. Do not place adhesive along the side with the slit.

4 Adhere panel 2 and panel 3 together by folding the 6" × 12" (15.25cm × 30.5cm) sheet in half.

5 Punch a half circle out of the fold with the slit.

Copic Markers

Copic Markers are perfect for coloring in stamped images. Copic Certified Instructor Sharon Harnist demonstrates the basics and gives us some tips and tricks for using these markers. The card design on page 114 makes beautiful use of this technique.

M A T E R I A L S

Stamp • Copic Markers • Cardstock • Ink • Silk ribbon glitter pen

1 Stamp the image with the Copic-safe dye ink onto the Copic-safe cardstock. Color the hydrangeas with the lightest base layer with a pink Copic Marker (R20).

2 Add shading definition to the pink hydrangeas with the darker pink marker (R22).

Copic Marker Numbering System

- The letter indicates the color family.
- The first digit indicates the color saturation. Colors that are 00s, 10s or 20s will be more vibrant, while numbers in the 70s, 80s and 90s range have more gray added and are close to the neutral/earthy end of the color spectrum. Note: E (Earth) tones don't necessarily follow this rule.
- The second digit indicates the lightness or darkness of the color saturation: 0 being the lightest and 9 being the darkest.

Copic Marker Tips

Because Copic Markers are alcohol-based, they will react with and smear an alcohol or solvent-based stamping ink. Copic-safe dye inks include: Memento (Tsukineko), Adirondack Pitch Black (Ranger Industries), and Palette (Stewart Superior).

Copic Markers can bleed or spread farther than the image you are coloring on many cardstocks. Some Copic-safe cardstock includes: Classic Crest (Neenah), Choice (Taylored Expressions), Pure Luxury (Gina K Designs), and white cardstock (Georgia-Pacific).

3 Color the smallest leaves with the lightest green marker (YG01) and the larger leaves with the middle shade of green marker (YG03).

4 Add shading definition to the larger leaves with a darker green marker (YG63).

5 Color the berries with a lighter blue marker (B21); dot the centers of the berries with a darker blue marker (B23).

6 Color the center of the jug and the bottom band with the lightest earth tone marker (E50). Color the rest of the jug and the accent center lettering with the middle earth tone marker (E31).

7 Add shading to the left side and the bottom of the jug with a darker earth tone marker (E35); add shadow to the left side and bottom of the jug with the W1 marker.

8 Using the lightest markers in each color family, go back and lightly blend the shading together on the hydrangeas (R20), large leaves (YG03) and jug (E31). Accent the hydrangeas with the ink glitter pen.

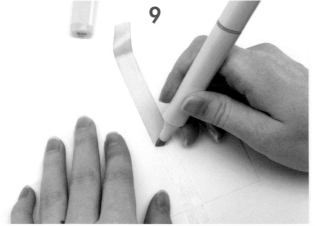

9 Color the white silk ribbon with the R20 marker. Set the ribbon aside to allow it to dry.

10 Color the embossed edge of the die-cut paper with an E47 marker.

Birthdays

Birthdays happen every year whether we want them to or not. For the enthusiastic child, try a card that features lots of color and a number for their special age. For an adult, consider a card with humor or sincerity to let them know that you're thinking of them on their special day.

Cupcake Card

by Kimber McGray

Who doesn't love a cupcake for their birthday?
This basic card design can be used for any birthday celebration, no matter the age.

1 Fold a 5½" × 8½" (14cm × 21.5cm) piece of tan cardstock in half to create a 4¼" × 5½" (10.75cm × 14cm) standard A2 card.

2 Cut a 3" × 5½" (7.5cm × 14cm) piece of yellow patterned paper and adhere it to the front of the card. With a scallop border punch, punch the edge of a green piece of patterned paper to create a 5½" × ¾" (14cm × 2cm) strip and adhere it to the front edge of the card, hanging it over the edge a bit.

3 Tie a piece of purple ribbon around the front of the card between the 2 pieces of patterned paper.

4 To create the cupcake, punch a 3" (7.5cm) circle out of pink patterned paper. Cut off the bottom third of the circle and scallop the edge with scissors. The cupcake base is a 2" (5cm) square with rounded corners. Layer on your card front and draw a black border around the edges with a pen.

5 For the cupcake pick, trim a 1" (2.5cm) strip of patterned paper, wrap it around the top of a straight pin and adhere it closed. Cut a triangle into the closed end. Pierce the pin through the top of the cupcake.

SUPPLIES

Cardstock (Core'dinations) • Patterned paper (Jillibean Soup, Bella Blvd) Punch (Stampin' Up!) • Ribbon (May Arts) • Straight pin • (Fiskars) • Pen (Martha Stewart Crafts) • Scissors • Adhesive of choice

16th Birthday for Boy Card

by Kimber McGray

Quick, easy, simple and straight to the point is the best way to go with wishing your favorite sixteen-year-old a happy birthday on such a momentous occasion.

1 Fold a 5½" × 7¼" (14cm × 18.5cm) piece of patterned paper at 3" (7.5cm) to create a 5½" × 4¼" (14cm × 10.75cm) standard A2 card. The front flap will be 3" (7.5cm) and the base will be 4¼" (10.75cm).

2 Clip a ticket stub on the front flap of the card with a small paper clip.

3 Handcut or die cut the number "16" from black cardstock and adhere it to the front of the ticket stub.

SUPPLIES

Cardstock (Core'dinations)
Patterned paper (Pebbles Inc.)
Clip (Stampin' Up!)
Ticket (Jenni Bowlin Studio)
Die cuts (QuicKutz)
Adhesive of choice

Baby's 1st Birthday Card

by Kimber McGray

A premade dimensional embellishment makes quick work of this card. Simply adding some soft touches, like dry embossing and a satin ribbon, sweetens the card to celebrate baby's first year.

1 Fold a 5½" × 8½" (14cm × 21.5cm) piece of gold cardstock in half to create a 5½" × 4¼" (14cm × 10.75cm) standard A2 card. Cut a 4" × 5¼" (10.25cm × 13.25cm) piece of cream cardstock and run it through an embossing machine to create a dotted background, and adhere it to the front of the card.

2 Tie a bow in a piece of blue ribbon, and attach it to the card front with the bow at the far right. Wrap the left end of the ribbon around the back and the right end around to the inside of the card and attach both ends. Then place the premade dimensional embellishment on the front of the card.

3 Handcut or die cut a "1" from coordinating patterned paper, and adhere it to the card front.

SUPPLIES

Cardstock (Stampin' Up!)
Patterned paper (Cosmo Cricket)
Ribbon (Papertrey Ink)
Sticker (Paperbilities)
Embossing folder (Provo Craft Cuttlebug)
Scissors
Adhesive of choice

Happy Birthday Candle Card

by Sarah Hodgkinson

One candle tells you exactly what this card is all about. Follow this design and extend a simple birthday wish to a loved one.

1 Begin with a kraft card (standard size 4¼" × 5½" [10.75cm × 14cm]).

2 Adhere a die-cut scalloped circle to the center of the card.

3 Cut a circle from green patterned paper to fit the center of the die-cut circle, ink the edges and adhere the circle to the front of the card.

4 Adhere the birthday candle to the front of the card with an adhesive dot.

5 Wrap a piece of twine around the candle and tie it into a bow.

6 With a pen and a circle template, draw 3 overlapping circles around the green circle.

7 Attach the brad to the front of the card.

SUPPLIES

Cardstock (Jillibean Soup)
Patterned paper (Jillibean Soup)
Twine (Jillibean Soup)
Brad (Bazzill Basics)
Die cut (Jillibean Soup)
Ink (Tsukineko)
Circle template (Creative Memories)
Birthday candle
Pen
Adhesive of choice
Adhesive dot
Scissors

Birthday Presents Card

By Laura Vegas

Bright and cheery gifts greet the birthday child to wish a happy birthday!

1 Fold a 5½" × 8½" (14cm × 21.5cm) piece of white cardstock in half to create a standard 4¼" × 5½" (10.75cm × 14cm) card base.

2 Cut a piece of blue patterned paper to 4" × 2" (10.25cm × 5cm) and adhere it to the front of the card.

3 Cut a piece of red patterned paper to 4" × 3¼" (10.25cm × 8.25cm) and adhere it to the front of the card.

4 Cut a strip of yellow patterned paper to 4" × ½" (10.25cm × 1.25cm) and adhere it to the middle of the card where the papers meet.

5 Add a 4" × ¼" (10.25cm × 6mm) long piece of green cardstock that has been punched with a decorative border punch to the center of the card front.

6 Attach the brads to the edges of the yellow patterned paper.

7 Adhere the present die cuts with foam adhesive to the front of the card.

SUPPLIES

Cardstock (Bazzill Basics)

Patterned paper (My Mind's Eye, KI Memories, Jillibean Soup)

Stickers (BasicGrey)

Brads (Making Memories)

Punch (Stampin' Up!)

Paper trimmer or scissors

Adhesive of choice

Foam adhesive

Robot Birthday Card

By Lynn Ghahary

Even in robot-speak, the birthday message comes across loud and clear with this design.

1 Fold a 5½" × 8½" (14cm × 21.5cm) piece of orange cardstock in half to create a standard 4¼" × 5½" (10.75cm × 14cm) card base. Round the corners of the base card.

2 Cut a 5½" × 2" (14cm × 5cm) piece of blue patterned paper and adhere it to the front of the card.

3 Cut a 3½" × 4½" (9cm × 11.5cm) piece of tan patterned paper, round the corners and adhere it to the front of the card.

4 Poke holes in the cardstock and hand stitch the green x's around the edge of the tan patterned paper.

5 Cut out the starburst design from the green patterned paper and adhere it to the front of the card.

6 Adhere a robot sticker to the front of the card with foam adhesive.

SUPPLIES

Cardstock (Bazzill Basics)
Patterned paper (Pebbles Inc.)
Stickers (Pebbles Inc.)
Punch (EK Success)
Floss (Bazzill Basics)
Robot sticker (Pebbles, Inc.)
Adhesive of choice
Foam adhesives
Robot sticker

! **See Hand Stitching on page 12 to learn how to achieve this attractive effect.**

Floral Birthday Card

by Kelly Goree

The sugary sweet colors and light-hearted flowers greet the birthday girl with cheer.

1 Fold a 5½" × 8½" (14cm × 21.5cm) piece of yellow cardstock in half to create a standard 4¼" × 5½" (10.75cm × 14cm) card base.

2 Cut a 5¼" × 4" (13.25cm × 10.25cm) piece of dotted pink patterned paper and adhere it to the front of the card with foam adhesive.

3 Cut a 5¼" × 1¼" (13.25cm × 3.25cm) piece of solid pink patterned paper and layer over the dotted pink piece of patterned paper.

4 Cut three 5½" × ¼" (14cm × 6mm) strips of coordinating patterned paper and layer them over the seam of the 2 pink papers. Use a decorative edge punch on one of the strips for a soft edge.

5 Cut circles from a green piece and a blue piece of patterned paper. The green circle should be 3" (7.5cm) wide and the blue circle should be 2" (5cm) wide. Adhere them to the front of the card and trim off part of the circles so they lay flush against the border stripes.

6 Using pens, draw faux stitching lines along the edges of the papers.

SUPPLIES

Cardstock (Bazzill Basics)

Patterned paper (BasicGrey)

Stickers (BasicGrey)

Gemstones (BasicGrey)

Ink (ColorBox by Clearsnap)

Punches (Marvy)

Pens

Paper trimmer or scissors

Adhesive of choice

! **See Faux Stitching on page 12 to learn how to embellish your cards with this attractive technique.**

Sweet Birthday Cupcake Card

by Melissa Phillips

What's a girl to love more: the sparkle of gemstones or a pink frosted cupcake? Give her both with this sweet birthday cupcake card.

1 Fold an 8½" × 4½" (21.5cm × 11.5cm) piece of cream cardstock in half to create a 4½" × 4¼" (11.5cm × 10.75cm) card base.

2 Cut a piece of tan patterned paper to 4" × 4¼" (10.25cm × 10.75cm) and adhere it to the font of the card.

3 Cut a piece of pink patterned paper to 3¾" × 4" (9.5cm × 10.25cm) and layer it over the tan piece of patterned paper and adhere it.

4 Machine stitch along the borders of the layered papers.

5 Adhere a die-cut oval to the center of the card.

6 Stamp cupcake images on 2 different pieces of patterned paper. Cut the images out and adhere them to the front of the card.

7 Embellish the card with gemstones, flowers, ribbon and buttons.

SUPPLIES

Cardstock (Papertrey Ink)

Patterned paper (Melissa Frances)

Stamps (Papertrey Ink)

Stickers (Melissa Frances)

Ribbon (Papertrey Ink)

Buttons (Papertrey Ink)

Gemstones (Zva Creative)

Ink (Papertrey Ink)

Paper trimmer or scissors

Adhesive of choice

Sewing machine

Happy 4th Birthday Card for a Boy

by Paula Gilarde

Little boys like to shout their ages from the rooftops when they are young. Help them celebrate every year like it's the best.

1 Fold a 5½" × 8½" (14cm × 21.5cm) piece of black cardstock in half to create a standard 4¼" × 5½" (10.75cm × 14cm) card base.

2 Cut a piece of number patterned paper to 4" × 5" (10.25cm × 12.75cm) and adhere it to the front of the card.

3 Add a decorative border sticker to a piece of black cardstock and trim along the sticker to leave a small black border. Adhere it to the center of the card.

4 Repeat the same technique with a robot scalloped circle sticker and trim around the edge to leave a thin black border. Adhere it to the front of the card with foam adhesive.

5 Paint the chipboard number with blue paint and adhere it to the front of the card.

Pink Bling Girly Birthday Card

by Kimber McGray

Wrap up a card for your favorite little girl with pink ribbon and gemstones.

1 Fold a 4¼" × 9½" (10.75cm × 24.25cm) piece of pink patterned paper in half to create a 4¼" × 4¾" (10.75cm × 12cm) card. Round the bottom corners of the card.

2 Tie a bow in a piece of polka dot ribbon, and attach it to the card front. Wrap the top end of the ribbon around the back and the bottom end around to the inside of the card and attach both ends.

3 Add gems to the front of the card.

4 Slide the pins and the metal clip into the knot of the bow. Secure them with an adhesive dot behind the top of the pins.

5 Draw faux stitching lines around the card edge with a white gel pen.

SUPPLIES

Patterned paper (KI Memories)

Ribbon (Berwick Offray)

Gems (Zva Creative)

Metal clip (Doodlebug Design)

Pins (Fancy Pants Designs)

Punch (We R Memory Keepers)

Pen (Uni-ball Signo)

Adhesive dots

! **Page 12 features the Faux Stitching technique that is the base of this card.**

40th Birthday Card

by Jennifer Buck

For some milestone birthdays, you need to have a sense of
humor to get through the changing of ages.

1 Fold a 4½" × 8½" (11.5cm × 21.5cm) piece of blue cardstock in half to create a standard 4¼" × 5½" (10.75cm × 14cm) card base.

2 Stamp the image on the white cardstock and color it with the markers.

3 Layer the image on the blue cardstock.

4 Cut a piece of patterned paper to 5" × 3¾" (12.75cm × 9.5cm) and adhere it to the front of the card.

5 Adhere the stamped image piece to the front of the card with foam adhesive.

6 Embellish the card with dew drops, chipboard numbers and ribbon.

SUPPLIES

Cardstock (Papertrey Ink)

Stamp (Gina K Designs)

Ribbon (May Arts)

Patterned paper (American Crafts)

Markers (Copic Markers)

Ink (Papertrey Ink)

Dew drops (The Robin's Nest)

Paper trimmer or scissors

Adhesive of choice

Foam adhesive

Balloon Trio Birthday Card

by Kandis Smith

Up, up and away! Celebrate another year by lifting the spirits of the birthday boy or girl!

1 Fold a piece of 5½" × 11" (14cm × 28cm) piece of orange cardstock to create a 5½" × 5½" (14cm × 14cm) card base.

2 Cut a 4½" × 4½" (11.5cm × 11.5cm) piece of striped patterned paper and adhere it to the center of the card front. Machine stitch around the border.

3 Cut a 1½" × 4½" (3.75cm × 11.5cm) piece of dotted patterned paper and adhere it to the center of the card front and attach with 2 brads.

4 Stamp balloon images on coordinating cardstock. Cut them out and adhere them to the front of the card with foam adhesive.

5 Embellish the card with ribbons and glitter glue.

SUPPLIES

Cardstock (Core'dinations)

Stamps (Hero Arts)

Ribbon (Maya Road and Michaels)

Brads (Imaginisce)

Patterned paper (Imaginisce, BoBunny Press)

Glitter glue (Ranger Industries)

Paper trimmer or scissors

Adhesive of choice

Foam adhesive

Sewing machine

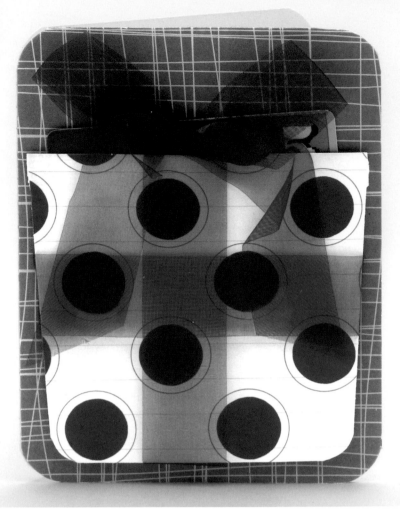

Pretty Present Gift Card Holder

by Kimber McGray

Make the card the gift by tucking a gift card into the present on the front of this card.

1 Fold a piece of 5½" × 8½" (14cm × 21.5cm) white cardstock in half to create a standard 5½" × 4¼" (14cm × 10.75cm) card. Round the corners.

2 Cut a 5½" × 4¼" (14cm × 10.75cm) piece of green patterned paper and adhere it to the front of the card. Round the corners.

3 Cut a 4" × 4" (10.25cm × 10.25cm) piece of polka dot patterned paper to look like a birthday gift. Adhere it to the front of the card with foam adhesive around the 3 edges only.

4 Add ribbon to the front of the birthday gift.

5 Tie a ribbon around a gift card and tie it into a bow. Slide the gift card behind the present with the bow sticking out the top.

S U P P L I E S

Cardstock (Bazzill Basics)

Patterned paper (Creative Imaginations, Cosmo Cricket, BoBunny Press)

Ribbon (May Arts)

Punch (Stampin' Up! and We R Memory Keepers)

Paper trimmer or scissors

Adhesive of choice

Foam adhesive

Purse Gift Card Holder

by Kimber McGray

What does a girl want for her birthday? To go shopping, of course! Fill
this purse with a gift card for her to spend as she wishes.

1 Fold a 4¼" × 11" (10.75cm × 28cm) piece of cream cardstock in half to create a standard 4¼" × 5½" (10.75cm × 14cm) card base.

2 Cut a 5" × 4" (12.75cm × 10.25cm) piece of scalloped patterned paper, tie a ribbon around the bottom edge and adhere it to the front of the card.

3 Place a scrap piece of cardstock on the back of the chipboard purse. Trim around the edge to leave a thin border. Adhere it to the front of the card with foam adhesive around 3 of the edges.

4 Add a button to the front of the chipboard purse.

5 Slide a gift card behind the purse.

SUPPLIES

Cardstock (Core'dinations)
Patterned paper (My Mind's Eye)
Chipboard (My Mind's Eye)
Button (Stampin' Up!)
Punch (Stampin' Up!)
Ribbon (May Arts)
Paper trimmer or scissors
Adhesive of choice
Foam adhesive

Candy Bar Wrapper

by Lisa Dorsey

Wrap up a chocolate bar for a quick and easy gift for kids of all ages.

Supplies:

Cardstock (Core'dinations, Bazzill Basics); patterned paper (We R Memory Keepers); punch (EK Success); die (Sizzix); pen (Sharpie)

Chinese Take Out Gift Box

by Lisa Dorsey

What a fun way to present a gift to the birthday boy or girl. Decorating a Chinese take-out container with patterned papers that coordinate with your card is a great way to present a present.

Supplies:

Patterned paper (BasicGrey, We R Memory Keepers); ribbon (Wrights); buttons (Papertrey Ink); box (Westrim Crafts)

1st Birthday Card
by Kim Moreno

1st Birthday Card
by Vivian Masket

Supplies:

Cardstock (Core'dinations); patterned paper (Pebbles Inc.); ribbon (Pebbles Inc.); stickers (Pebbles Inc, American Crafts); punch (Martha Stewart Crafts); buttons (Fancy Pants Designs); twine (Jillibean Soup)

Supplies:

Cardstock (Bazzill Basics); pattern paper (Sassafras Lass); chipboard (Sassafras Lass); foam numbers (American Crafts); punch (EK Success)

Bike Birthday Card
by Jennifer Buck

13th Birthday Card
by Summer Fullerton

Supplies:

Cardstock (Papertrey Ink); patterned paper (Cosmo Cricket); ribbon (Papertrey Ink); chipboard (Cosmo Cricket)

Supplies:

Cardstock (Jillibean Soup, Bazzill Basics); patterned paper (Jillibean Soup); rhinestones (Kaisercraft); twine (Jillibean Soup); alphas (Jillibean Soup); paint (Making Memories); button (SEI); brads (BasicGrey); punch (EK Success)

5th Birthday Card
by Kimber McGray

Supplies:

Cardstock (Bazzill Basics); patterned paper (BasicGrey, Jillibean Soup, Making Memories); stickers (Martha Stewart Crafts); punch (Stampin' Up!, Marvy, We R Memory Keepers)

30th Birthday Card
by Kimber McGray

Supplies:

Cardstock (Jillibean Soup); die cut (Creative Imaginations); chipboard (Sassafras Lass); pen (Uni-ball Signo); twill (Creative Impressions)

Motorcycle Birthday Card
by Kimber McGray

Supplies:

Cardstock (Core'dinations); patterned paper (BasicGrey, Jillibean Soup, BoBunny Press); chipboard (My Mind's Eye); ink (ColorBox by Clearsnap); punch (We R Memory Keepers, Fiskars); floss (DMC)

Rock On Hand Birthday Card
by Kimber McGray

Supplies:

Patterned paper (October Afternoon, BoBunny Press); gemstones (Zva Creative); punch (Fiskars); tag (office supply store)

Patchwork Birthday Card
by Kimber McGray

Supplies:

Patterned paper (Making Memories); punch (Fiskars, We R Memory Keepers); twine (Jillibean Soup); gemstones (Zva Creative)

Cupcake Birthday Card
by Kimber McGray

Supplies:

Cardstock (Core'dinations); patterned paper (American Crafts, October Afternoon); chipboard (Maya Road); embossing powder (American Crafts); button (Stampin' Up!); ribbon (Creative Impressions); punch (We R Memory Keepers); embossing folder (Provo Craft Cuttlebug); embroidery floss (DMC)

See page 122 for a basic sketch of this card.

Princess Crowns Birthday Card
by Kimber McGray

Supplies:

Cardstock (Core'dinations); patterned paper (KI Memories, Pink Paislee, Reminisce, Jenni Bowlin Studio); gemstones (Heidi Swapp); pins (Maya Road); punch (EK Success); tags (office supply store)

Girly Birthday Card
by Kimber McGray

Supplies:

Cardstock (Core'dinations); patterned paper (BoBunny Press); gemstones (Zva Creative); flowers (Making Memories); punch (We R Memory Keepers)

Hello Kitty Little Girl Birthday Card
by Kimber McGray

See page 122 for a basic sketch of this card.

Supplies:

Cardstock (Core'dinations); patterned paper (Sandylion Sticker Designs); gemstones (Zva Creative); embossing folder (Provo Craft Cuttlebug)

Birthday Hat Card
by Kimber McGray

Supplies:

Patterned Paper (Bella Blvd); brad (Queen & Co.); ribbon (Bazzill Basics); punches (EK Success)

45th Birthday Card
by Kimber McGray

Supplies:

Cardstock (Bazzill Basics); patterned paper (BoBunny Press, Jillibean Soup); stamp (Stampin' Up!); ribbon (Making Memories); markers (Copic); punch (Stampin' Up!)

Star Birthday Card
by Kimber McGray

Supplies:

Cardstock (Core'dinations); patterned paper (Jillibean Soup); button (Making Memories); ribbon (Making Memories); stickers (Sassafras Lass); punches (Stampin' Up!, We R Memory Keepers)

Robot Boy Birthday Card
by Kimber McGray

Supplies:

Cardstock (Core'dinations); patterned paper (Jillibean Soup); stamp (Stampin' Up!); ink (Brilliance by Tsukineko); markers (Copic); ribbon (Stampin' Up!); punches (We R Memory Keepers, EK Success)

Butterfly Birthday Card
by Kimber McGray

Supplies:

Patterned Paper (Studio Calico, BoBunny Press); buttons (Stampin' Up!); punch (Stampin' Up!); clip (Making Memories)

Orange and Black Butterfly Birthday Card
by Kimber McGray

Buzz and Bloom Butterfly Birthday Card
by Kimber McGray

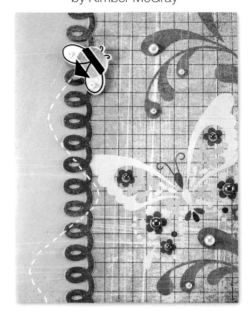

Supplies:

Cardstock (Jillibean Soup); patterned paper (BoBunny Press, Jillibean Soup); brads (Sassafras Lass, BasicGrey); die cut (Heidi Swapp); punch (Stampin' Up!); ribbon (Making Memories)

Supplies:

Patterned paper (BasicGrey); gemstones (Zva Creative); pen (Uni-ball Signo)

8th Birthday Card
by Kimber McGray

Big Star Birthday Card
by Kimber McGray

Army Birthday Card
by Kimber McGray

Supplies:

Cardstock (Core'dinations); patterned paper (BoBunny Press, SEI, October Afternoon); chipboard (Sassafras Lass); buttons and twine (craft supply store)

Supplies:

Patterned paper (October Afternoon and BoBunny Press); die-cut cardstock (KI Memories); gemstones (Zva Creative); die-cut star (Provo Craft Cricut)

Supplies:

Cardstock (Jillibean Soup); rub-on (Hambly Studios); ribbon (Making Memories); button (Stampin' Up!); stamp (American Crafts); ink (ColorBox by Clearsnap); tag (Paper Reflections); twine (Jillibean Soup); staples

2

Season's Greetings

No matter what wintertime holiday you celebrate, keep it simple and remember your reason for the season. Send greetings of snowmen and snowflakes, candles aglow or Santa in his sleigh to your friends and family members. This is the most wonderful time of the year to deliver handmade cards.

Christmas Photo Card

by Summer Fullerton

When you have a lot of cards to make, use up scraps of coordinating paper and photos of your smiling family for easy-to-duplicate cards.

1 Fold a 6" × 12" (15.25cm × 30.5cm) piece of kraft cardstock in half to create a 6" × 6" (15.25cm × 15.25cm) card.

2 Cut 3 pieces of coordinating patterned paper, one 3" × 3" (7.5cm × 7.5cm), the next 3" × 2½" (7.5cm × 6.25cm), and the third piece 2½" × 5½" (6.25cm × 14cm). Adhere the papers to the front of card base.

3 Mat the photo on a piece of white cardstock and adhere it to the front of the card.

4 Place 2 triangles of blue cardstock in the corners of the photos to create photo corners, and attach them with matching brads.

SUPPLIES

Cardstock (Bazzill Basics)

Patterned paper (Jillibean Soup, October Afternoon)

Brads (BasicGrey)

Family photo

Paper trimmer or scissors

Adhesive of choice

Rustic Christmas Card

by Sarah Hodgkinson

Sarah topped the corrugated numbers with a bit of holiday snow and glitter to give this card a seasonal flair.

1 Fold a 5½" × 8½" (14cm × 21.5cm) piece of kraft cardstock to create a standard 5½" × 4¼" (14cm × 10.75cm) card base.

2 Cut a piece of white cardstock to 5" × 3¾" (12.75cm × 9.5cm). Round the corners and distress the edges. Adhere it to the front of the card base.

3 Cut a piece of red embossed cardstock to 4¾" × 3½" (12cm × 9cm), round the corners and distress the edges. Lightly sand the top and adhere it to the front of card base.

4 Stamp the images on the kraft cardstock. Cut them out and adhere them to the front of the card.

5 Wrap the twine around the front of the card and tie it into a bow.

6 Edge the numbers in clear-drying glue and sprinkle them with ultrafine glitter. Let the numbers dry and adhere them to the card front with foam adhesive.

SUPPLIES

Cardstock (Core'dinations, Jillibean Soup)

Numbers (Jillibean Soup)

Punch (We R Memory Keepers)

Twine (Jillibean Soup)

Ultrafine glitter (MultiCrafts & Gifts, Inc.)

Stamps (Unity Stamp Company)

Ink (Tsukineko)

Paper trimmer or scissors

Adhesive of choice

Clear-drying glue

Foam adhesive

Kwanzaa Card

by Stacey Kingman

Stacey used the colors of Kwanzaa in the colors of her candles; the tradition of placing the candles in a wooden base is reflected in her clever use of woodgrain patterned paper.

1 Fold a 6" × 6" (15.25cm × 15.25cm) piece of ivory cardstock in half to create a 3" × 6" (7.5cm × 15.25cm) card base.

2 Cut a ½" × 5¾" (1.25cm × 14.5cm) strip of woodgrain patterned paper and adhere it to the front of the card.

3 Cut scraps of red, green and black patterned papers to create candles and adhere them to the front of your card.

4 Machine stitch around the edges of all the paper strips.

5 Embellish the candles with gemstones.

SUPPLIES

Cardstock (Prism Papers)

Patterned paper (October Afternoon)

Gemstones (Kaisercraft)

Paper trimmer or scissors

Adhesive of choice

Sewing machine

Menorah Hanukkah Card

by Sherry Wright

Sherry expresses the meaning of the card and the feeling of the season by pairing blues and creams with the warmth of the yellow.

1 Fold a 5¼" × 10½" (13.25cm × 26.5cm) piece of cream cardstock in half to create a 5¼" × 5¼" (13.25cm × 13.25cm) square card base.

2 Cut a 5¼" × 5¼" (13.25cm × 13.25cm) piece of blue patterned paper to cover the front of the card base.

3 Cut a 5" × 5" (12.75cm × 12.75cm) piece of black patterned paper and adhere it to the center of the card front.

4 Cut a 4¾" × 4¾" (12cm × 12cm) piece of cream patterned paper, ink the edges and adhere it to the center of the card front.

5 Cut a piece of blue patterned paper into a 3¼" (8.25cm) circle, ink the edges and adhere it to the front of the card.

6 Handcut scraps of paper to create the menorah. Embellish the candles with gemstones for candle flames.

SUPPLIES

Cardstock (BoBunny Press)

Patterned paper (BoBunny Press)

Gemstones (BoBunny Press)

Punch (McGill)

Ink (Clearsnap, Inc.)

Paper trimmer or scissors

Adhesive of choice

Merry Little Christmas Card

by Lynn Ghahary

Lynn used a coordinating set of patterned paper and embellishments to create a cute, quick and easy card.

1 Fold a 4¼" × 11" (10.75cm × 28cm) piece of blue cardstock in half to create a 4¼" × 5½" (10.75cm × 14cm) standard card base.

2 Cut two 1" × 5½" (2.5cm × 14cm) pieces of reindeer patterned paper and adhere them to the front of the card base. Round the bottom corners of the card.

3 Cut two ¼" × 5½" (6mm × 14cm) pieces of green patterned paper and trim them with decorative edge scissors or a punch. Adhere them to the front of the card.

4 Cut two ¼" × 5½" (6mm × 14cm) pieces of striped patterned paper and adhere them to the front of the card.

5 Cut a 2½" (6.25cm) white circle and adhere it to the front of the card.

6 Embellish the card with chipboard pieces and epoxy stickers.

SUPPLIES

Cardstock (Core'dinations)

Patterned paper (BasicGrey)

Chipboard (BasicGrey)

Stickers (BasicGrey)

Punches (EK Success)

Decorative scissors (Fiskars)

Paper trimmer or scissors

Adhesive of choice

Winter Birds Holiday Card

by Kim Moreno

Kim used the design in a piece of patterned paper as the main source to embellish her card. Simply cutting out printed designs can make for fun embellishments.

1 Fold an 8½" × 4¼" (21.5cm × 10.75cm) piece of cardstock in half to create a 4¼" × 4¼" (10.75cm × 10.75cm) square card.

2 Cut a 3¾" × 3" (9.5cm × 7.5cm) piece of embossed red cardstock, round the corners and adhere it to the front of the card.

3 Tear pieces of white cardstock to create the hills and adhere them to the front of the card.

4 Tie a bow in a piece of ribbon, and attach it to the card front at the bottom. Wrap the left end of the ribbon around the back and the right end around to the inside of the card, and attach both ends.

5 Cut out pieces of the patterned paper and adhere them to the front of the card.

6 Punch 2 snowflakes and adhere them to the front of the card. Embellish with gemstones.

SUPPLIES

Cardstock (Core'dinations)

Patterned paper (Jillibean Soup)

Ribbon (Jillibean Soup)

Punch (Martha Stewart Crafts, Creative Memories)

Gemstones (Kaisercraft)

Paper trimmer or scissors

Adhesive of choice

Christmas Tree Pennant Card

by Jennifer Buck

Jennifer turned a chipboard pennant piece upside down to create a Christmas tree.

1 Fold an 8" × 10" (20.5cm × 25.5cm) piece of kraft cardstock in half to create an 8" × 5" (20.5cm × 12.75cm) card base.

2 Hand stitch around the edge of the card.

3 Cover the chipboard pennant with patterned paper. Trim the excess paper with the craft knife.

4 Tie the ribbon and adhere it to the top of the pennant.

5 Embellish the tree with a sticker and buttons.

SUPPLIES

Cardstock (Papertrey Ink)
Patterned paper (Cosmo Cricket)
Chipboard (Jenni Bowlin Studio)
Buttons (Papertrey Ink)
Ribbon (May Arts)
Ink (Papertrey Ink)
Embroidery floss (DMC)
Stitching guide
Foam mat
Needle
Paper piercer
Craft knife
Adhesive of choice

Music Note Poinsettia Christmas Card

by Kimber McGray

The sound of holiday music on a stamped poinsettia card sings Merry Christmas for all to hear.

1 Fold a 5½" × 8½" (14cm × 21.5cm) piece of kraft cardstock in half to create a standard 5½" × 4¼" (14cm × 10.75cm) card base.

2 Stamp the background image on the kraft card base with watermark ink.

3 Machine stitch a border around the perimeter of the card front.

4 Ink the edges of the scallop canvas sticker and adhere it to card front. Use freehand faux stitching with a black pen to create a circle boarder on the canvas sticker.

5 Stamp the flower image on 1 piece of green cardstock and 2 pieces of white cardstock. Cut out the different layers and reassemble them to create a dimensional paper-pieced flower.

6 Add red pearls to the top of the flower and adhere the flower to the front of the card.

See Paper Piecing on page 16 and Faux Stitching on page 12 to learn how to embellish your creations with handmade touches.

SUPPLIES

Kraft card (Jillibean Soup)

Cardstock (Core'dinations, Papertrey Ink)

Stamp (Unity Stamp Company, Stampabilities)

Canvas sticker (Technique Tuesday)

Watermark ink (Memento, ColorBox, VersaMark)

Pearls (Kaisercraft)

Paper trimmer or scissors

Adhesive of choice

Sewing machine

Scallop Punch Christmas Tree Card

by Paula Gilarde

Border punches are not just for a decorative touch. Paula used them to create branches on her pine tree. Perfect for some quick texture.

1 Fold a 5½" × 8½" (14cm × 21.5cm) piece of cardstock in half to create a standard 5½" × 4¼" (14cm × 10.75cm) card base.

2 Cut a rectangle of red embossed cardstock and adhere it to the front of the card base.

3 Cut 2 oval shapes, one smaller from embossed paper, and one larger oval with scalloped edges. Attach the embossed oval on top of the scalloped oval. Use the gold leaf pen to embellish the edges of the scalloped oval. Attach the oval to the front of the card.

4 Cut a tree shape from scrap paper to use as a template.

5 Cut strips out of the various shades of green of cardstock. Punch the strips with a decorative border punch and adhere them to the tree template. Trim the excess paper away from the template.

6 Cut a scrap of brown cardstock to create a tree trunk. Adhere the trunk and tree to the ovals. Adhere the chipboard star to the top of the tree.

SUPPLIES

Cardstock (Core'dinations) • Chipboard (Scenic Route) • Punch (Fiskars) Die (Spellbinders) • Gold leaf pen (Elmer's) • Paper trimmer or scissors • Adhesive of choice

! **See the Punches technique on page 13 for instructions on making this cute tree creation.**

Santa Sleigh Gift Card

by Kimber McGray

Deliver a gift to a friend the same way Santa does—in his sleigh.

1 Fold a 7" × 10" (17.75cm × 25.5cm) piece of black card-stock in half to create a 5" × 7" (12.75cm × 17.75cm) card base.

2 Cut a 5½" × 4½" (14cm × 11.5cm) piece of cream patterned paper and adhere it to the front of the card.

3 Cut a strip of green patterned paper and punch it with a decorative border punch. Adhere it to the front of the card.

4 Handcut or die cut a 4" (10.25cm) sleigh image from both a piece of black cardstock and a piece of argyle patterned paper. Adhere them to the front of the card with foam adhesive around 3 of the edges, leaving the top of the sleigh open.

5 Embellish the card front with gemstones and ribbon trim.

6 Tie a ribbon around a gift card and slide it into the sleigh opening.

SUPPLIES

Cardstock (Bazzill Basics)
Patterned paper (Making Memories)
Die (Provo Craft Cricut)
Gemstones (Zva Creative)
Ribbon (May Arts, Bazzill Basics)
Punch (Stampin' Up!)
Paper trimmer or scissors
Adhesive of choice
Foam adhesive

Christmas Goodie Bag Topper

by Lisa Dorsey

Many of us like to give a gift of sweets to neighbors, teachers and friends. Placing a gift in a clear cellophane bag and topping it with a festive touch makes a great presentation.

Supplies:

Cardstock (Bazzill Basics); patterned paper (BasicGrey, Graphic 45); ribbon (May Arts, Jo-Ann Fabrics & Crafts); ink (ColorBox by Clearsnap); scallop blade (Fiskars); gemstones (BasicGrey)

Decorated Gift Card Tin

by Kimber McGray

Gift cards are easy gifts to give. Make them a bit more fun by decking out a metal tin with festive decorative tape for the holiday season.

Supplies:

Patterned paper (BoBunny Press); punch (Marvy), ink (ColorBox by Clearsnap); decorative tape (Making Memories); chipboard (Making Memories); twine (Jillibean Soup); tin (Archiver's)

Snowflake Card
by Sandy Allnock

Santa and Holly Card
by Sherry Wright

Oh Christmas Tree! Card
by Kandis Smith

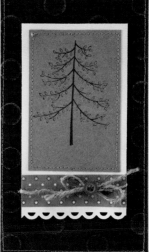

Supplies:

Cardstock (Georgia-Pacific, Beckett by Mohawk Fine Papers, Inc.); embossing folder (Sizzix); punch (Marvy, EK Success); miscellaneous ribbon and buttons

Supplies:

Patterned paper (BoBunny Press); ribbon (BoBunny Press); punch (Martha Stewart Crafts, McGill, Inc.); sticker (BoBunny Press)

Supplies:

Cardstock (Core'dinations, Provo Craft); stamps (Hero Arts); ink (Memories by Stewart Superior); patterned paper (Imaginisce); colored pencils (Prismacolor); twine (Jillibean Soup); punch (Fiskars); button (Making Memories)

Birdie Christmas Card
by Laura Vegas

Snowflake Dream Card
by Teza Hampton

Supplies:

Patterned paper (Jillibean Soup); ribbon (Jillibean Soup); chipboard (Lil' Davis Designs); button (Autumn Leaves); twine (Jillibean Soup); gemstone (Hero Arts); staples

Supplies:

Cardstock (Bazzill Basics); patterned paper (My Mind's Eye); dies (Spellbinders); die cut (Martha Stewart Crafts); brad (Making Memories); punch (Fiskars); embossing folder (Provo Craft Cuttlebug); gemstones (My Mind's Eye); twine (May Arts); ink (Ranger Industries); miscellaneous ribbon

Retro Christmas Tree Card
by Jenn Biederman

Home for the Holidays Card
by Melissa Phillips

Christmas Gifts Card
by Kelly Goree

Supplies:

Cardstock (DMD by Creativity, Inc.); patterned paper (BasicGrey); stamps (Purple Onion Designs); ink (Ranger Industries); gemstones (Hero Arts, BasicGrey); dies (Spellbinders); colored pencils (Prismacolor)

Supplies:

Cardstock (Papertrey Ink); patterned paper (BasicGrey); sticker (BasicGrey); resin embellishment (Melissa Frances); ribbon (Papertrey Ink); gemstones (Melissa Frances); ink (Ranger Industries)

Supplies:

Cardstock (Bazzill Basics); patterned paper (BasicGrey); chipboard (BasicGrey); ink (ColorBox by Clearsnap); punches (Fiskars)

Hanukkah Card
by Stacey Kingman

Juggling Santa Card
by Vivian Masket

Supplies:

Patterned paper (October Afternoon, BoBunny Press); gemstones (Zva Creative); punch (Fiskars); tag (office supply store)

Supplies:

Cardstock (Bazzill Basics); patterned paper (October Afternoon); stamp (October Afternoon); ink (StazOn by Tsukineko); gemstones (Kaisercraft, Doodlebug Design)

Snowman Card
by Kimber McGray

Supplies:

Cardstock (Bazzill Basics, Jillibean Soup); stamp (Cornish Heritage Farms); ink (Memento by Tsukineko); markers (Copic); punch (Stampin' Up!); embroidery floss (DMC)

Glitter Holly Card
by Kimber McGray

Supplies:

Cardstock (Bazzill Basics); patterned paper (Making Memories); leaves (Making Memories); ribbon (May Arts); brads (The Paper Company); ink (ColorBox by Clearsnap)

Cardinal in Tree Card
by Kimber McGray

Supplies:

Cardstock (Jillibean Soup); rub-on (Hambly Studios); sticker (Making Memories); stamp (Stampin' Up!); ink (Jo-Ann Craft Essentials); punch (EK Success)

Hanukkah Holiday Wishes Card
by Keri Lee Sereika

Supplies:

Cardstock (Prism Papers); stamps (Impression Obsession); ink (Memento by Tsukineko); patterned papers (Jenni Bowlin Studio); ribbon (May Arts); gemstones (Prima Marketing, Inc.); dies (Spellbinders); gold leafing pen (Krylon)

Menorah Eight Night Card
by Kimber McGray

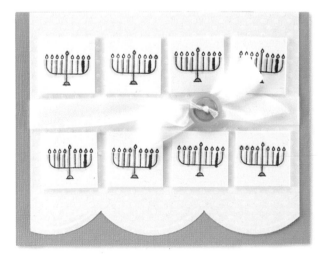

Supplies:

Cardstock (Bazzill Basics, Core'dinations); inchies (Inchie Arts); stamp (Stampin' Up!); ink (Memento by Tsukineko); punch (EK Success); button (Stampin' Up!); ribbon (Creative Impressions); markers (Copic)

White Holly Card
by Kimber McGray

Supplies:

Cardstock (Core'dinations); patterned paper (October Afternoon, Jillibean Soup); tape (Making Memories); stickers (Making Memories); brads (Queen & Co.); punch (We R Memory Keepers)

Snow Buddies Card
by Kimber McGray

Supplies:

Cardstock (Papertrey Ink); patterned paper (Pink Paislee); chipboard (My Mind's Eye); button (Stampin' Up!); twill (Wrights); embossing folder (Provo Craft Cuttlebug)

The Stockings Were Hung... Card
by Kimber McGray

Supplies:

Cardstock (Bazzill Basics); patterned paper (BoBunny Press, Doodlebug Design); stickers (Doodlebug Design); die cut (Doodlebug Design); button (Bazzill Basics); twill (May Arts)

Quiet Snowfall Card
by Kimber McGray

Supplies:

Patterned paper (Jillibean Soup, BasicGrey, BoBunny Press); punches (Stampin' Up!, We R Memory Keepers); gemstones (Zva Creative); brad (Making Memories); die cut (Provo Craft Cricut); ink (ColorBox by Clearsnap)

Three Wise Men Card
by Kimber McGray

Supplies:
Patterned paper (Jillibean Soup, BoBunny Press); stamps (Inkadinkado, Cornish Heritage Farms); ink (VersaMark, Brilliance by Tsukineko); glitter glue (Ranger Industries); embossing powder (American Crafts)

Retro Christmas Ornaments Card
by Kimber McGray

Supplies:
Cardstock (Papertrey Ink); ink (Brilliance by Tsukineko, Close To My Heart, ColorBox by Clearsnap); stamps (Unity Stamp Company); embossing folder (Provo Craft Cuttlebug); embossing powder (Stampin' Up!)

Holy Family Card
by Kimber McGray

Supplies:
Cardstock (Core'dinations, Papertrey Ink); patterned paper (October Afternoon, BoBunny Press); twill (Wrights); stamp (Inkadinkado); markers (Copic); ink (Memento by Tsukineko)

Coffee Gift Card Holder
by Kimber McGray

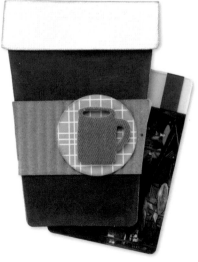

Supplies:
Cardstock (Core'dinations, Jillibean Soup); patterned paper (Jillibean Soup, BoBunny Press); chipboard (American Crafts); crimper (Fiskars); ink (ColorBox by Clearsnap); punch (EK Success)

Santa's Sleigh in the Sky Card
by Kimber McGray

Supplies:
Cardstock (Papertrey Ink); patterned paper (Creative Imaginations); transparency (Making Memories); rub-on (We R Memory Keepers); button (Stampin' Up!); ribbon (Creative Impressions); gemstones (Zva Creative)

3

Other Holidays

Almost every month gives us other holidays to send cards to our friends and family members. Share some love on Valentine's Day, honor a mother on Mother's Day. Let Dad know how much you love him on Father's Day. Congratulate a graduate in June as well. The fall brings us the excuse to send out ghoulish greetings and thankful blessings. There is always a reason to create a card throughout the year.

Sweetheart Card

by Melissa Phillips

The size of this cute card is perfectly suited for sliding a gift card inside for your sweetheart on Valentine's Day.

1 Fold a 5½" × 6" (14cm × 15.25cm) piece of red cardstock in half to create a 2¾" × 6" (7cm × 15.25cm) card base.

2 Cut a piece of apple patterned paper to 4½" × 2½" (11.5cm × 6.25cm). Ink its edges and adhere the paper to the front of the card.

3 Cut a piece of striped cardstock to 2½" × 1¼" (6.25cm × 3.25cm). Ink its edges and adhere the paper to the front of the card.

4 Tie a cream ribbon around the card and machine stitch in place.

5 Round the upper corner of the card.

6 Add the die-cut circle to the front of the card. Decorate the card with the buttons, gemstones and chipboard embellishments.

SUPPLIES

Cardstock (Papertrey Ink)

Patterned paper (October Afternoon, Graphic 45)

Die cuts (BasicGrey, My Mind's Eye)

Chipboard (Cosmo Cricket)

Gemstone (Melissa Frances)

Ink (Ranger Industries)

Miscellaneous buttons

Twill tape

Twine

Paper trimmer or scissors

Adhesive of choice

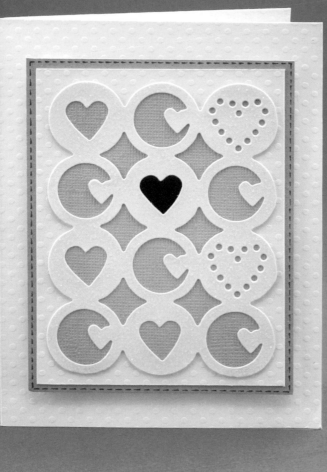

You Have My Heart
Valentine's Day Card

by Kelly Goree

Kelly layered a small piece of red cardstock behind one of the heart openings of the die-cut cardstock for a perfect punch of color to express the love in this card.

1 Fold an 8½" × 5½" (21.5cm × 14cm) piece of white embossed cardstock in half to create a standard 5½" × 4¼" (14cm × 10.75cm) card base.

2 Cut a 3½" × 4½" (9cm × 11.5cm) piece of kraft cardstock and adhere it to the front of the card with foam adhesive.

3 Cut a 3¼" × 5¼" (8.25cm × 13.25cm) piece of white embossed cardstock and adhere it to the front of the card.

4 Trim out a 3" × 4" (7.5cm × 10.25cm) piece of die-cut cardstock. Layer a piece of pink cardstock and a small piece of red cardstock under it. Adhere them to the front of the card.

5 With the pen, create faux stitching around the border of the kraft cardstock.

! See Faux Stitching on page 12 to learn how to do this cute technique.

SUPPLIES

Cardstock (Bazzill Basics, KI Memories)
Pen
Paper trimmer or scissors
Adhesive of choice
Foam adhesive

Frog Prince Valentine's Day Card

by Summer Fullerton

If you had to kiss a frog to find your prince, this would be the little guy that makes it worth the while.

1 Fold a 6" × 6" (15.25cm × 15.25cm) piece of pink cardstock in half to create a 3" × 6" (7.5cm × 15.25cm) card base.

2 Cut a blue piece of patterned paper to 2" × 6" (5cm × 15.25cm) and adhere it to the card front.

3 Cut a red piece of patterned paper to 1" × 6" (2.5cm × 15.25cm) and adhere it to the card front.

4 Tie a pink ribbon around the card front.

5 Punch a 3" (7.5cm) scalloped circle from a piece of white patterned paper and adhere it to the front of the card. Trim off the excess.

6 Stamp the frog image onto the kraft cardstock and then cut it out. Adhere it to the front of the card with foam adhesive.

7 Paint the chipboard crown pink, add gemstones and adhere them to the front of the card with foam adhesive.

SUPPLIES

Cardstock (Bazzill Basics, Jillibean Soup)

Stamp (Jillibean Soup)

Patterned papers (Pink Paislee)

Ribbon (Stampin' Up!)

Chipboard (Heidi Swapp)

Gemstones (me and my BIG ideas)

Punch (EK Success)

Ink (VersaFine by Tsukineko)

Paint (Making Memories)

Paper trimmer or scissors

Adhesive of choice

Foam adhesive

Shamrock Card

by Kimber McGray

By simply changing the color of one of the repeated images, the shamrock really stands out.

1 Score a 4¼" × 10" (10.75cm × 25.5cm) piece of green cardstock and fold it to create a 4½" × 5" (11.5cm × 12.75cm) card. Round the bottom corners with a corner rounder.

2 Cut a 4" × 4¾" (10.25cm × 12cm) piece of white cardstock and round the bottom corners with a corner rounder. Stamp the shamrock image 3 times in black ink and a 4th time with watermark ink onto this piece of cardstock.

3 Pour green embossing powder on the watermark image and shake off the excess. Heat the

embossing powder with the heat gun to set the powder.

4 Machine stitch a grid between the shamrocks. Add gems to the corners of the shamrocks.

5 Punch a scrap of yellow cardstock and adhere it to the back of the white cardstock.

6 Staple a piece of green striped ribbon to the edge of the white cardstock.

7 Adhere the embellished white cardstock piece to the front of the card with foam adhesive for dimension.

SUPPLIES

Cardstock (Core'dinations, Papertrey Ink) • Ink (Memento) • Watermark ink (VersaMark) • Gems (Zva Creative) • Ribbon (BasicGrey) • Punches (We R Memory Keepers, Stampin' Up!) • Embossing powder (American Crafts) • Heat gun • Paper trimmer or scissors • Adhesive of choice • Foam adhesive

! See page 122 for a basic sketch of this card.

See the Heat Embossing technique on page 14 that features this card design.

Easter Basket Full of Goodies Card

by Kimber McGray

You can put all your eggs in one basket when you are sending
this card to wish a friend Happy Easter.

1 Using the brown cardstock, handcut or die-cut a 4½" (11.5cm) Easter basket.

2 Cut 4 eggs (using the same dial size if using the Cricut) from different colors of patterned paper.

3 Score lines in the basket and lightly sand the top ridges.

4 Adhere the die-cut basket over a 5" × 5" (12.75cm × 12.75cm) folded white card. Cut away excess card using a craft knife along the edges of the brown basket.

5 Adhere the eggs inside the opening.

6 Tie a bow in a piece of ribbon, and attach it to the basket. Wrap the left end of the ribbon around the back and the right end around to the inside of the card, and attach both ends. Embellish the bow with a button.

SUPPLIES

Cardstock (Core'dinations)

Patterned paper (BasicGrey)

Die (Provo Craft Cricut)

Ribbon (Creative Impressions)

Button (Stampin' Up!)

Paper trimmer or scissors

Craft knife

Adhesive of choice

Mother's Day Trifold Card

by Kimber McGray

By simply scoring a piece of cardstock in different places instead of straight down the center, you can create a fun trifold card.

1 Score and fold a 4¼" × 10½" (10.75cm × 26.5cm) piece of patterned paper at 3" (7.5cm) and 7" (17.75cm). The final size of the folded card is 4¼" × 4" (10.75cm × 10.25cm). Round the corners on the font flap of the card.

2 Cut a coordinating piece of patterned paper to 4" × 3¾" (10.25cm × 9.5cm) and round the upper and lower corners on the right side. Adhere the paper to the front of the card, lining up the left edge to the fold.

3 Pierce holes around the borders of the layered papers and hand stitch with the embroidery floss.

4 Cut down a coordinating die cut and transparency to 4½" × 1¾" (11.5cm × 4.5cm) and adhere it to the front of the card.

5 Stamp the image on a piece of yellow patterned paper. Color it in with markers and add pearls.

6 Adhere the embellished, stamped image to the front of the card. Layer a die-cut frame to the top of the image and adhere it to the card front.

SUPPLIES

Patterned paper (BoBunny Press, BasicGrey) • Die cut (BasicGrey and Making Memories) • Gems (Zva Creative) • Stamp (Unity Stamp Company) • Markers (Copic) • Transparency (BasicGrey) • Punch (We R Memory Keepers) • Stitching guide (Bazzill Basics) • Foam mat • Needle • Paper piercer • Thread or embroidery floss • Paper trimmer or scissors • Adhesive of choice

! See the Hand Stitching technique on page 12 to learn the basics of this attractive embellishment.

Mother's Day Butterfly Card

by Kimber McGray

From the colors to the heart antennae on the butterfly, loves abounds
from this card that will suit any mother on Mother's Day.

1 Fold an 11" × 4¼" (28cm × 10.75cm) piece of cream cardstock in half to create a 4¼" × 5¼" (10.75cm × 13.25cm) standard A2 card.

2 Cut 3 different patterned papers of the same color family into pieces that measure: 1¼" × 5½" (3.25cm × 14cm) of the striped paper; 1¼" × 2½" (3.25cm × 6.25cm) of the polka dot paper; and 3¾" × 2½" (9.5cm × 6.25cm) of the pink paper.

3 Adhere the striped paper to the front of the card. Round 1 of the corners on the pink polka dot paper and adhere the paper to the front of the card. Tie a piece of white ribbon around the pink paper and tie into a bow before adhering the paper to the front of the card.

4 In the center of the bow, attach a die cut or punched butterfly. Add 2 straight pins to create antennae.

SUPPLIES

Cardstock (Core'dinations)

Patterned paper (Anna Griffin, SEI)

Die cut (K&Company)

Ribbon (Creative Impressions)

Straight pins (Fancy Pants Designs)

Punch (EK Success)

Paper trimmer or scissors

Adhesive of choice

! See page 122 for a basic sketch of this card.

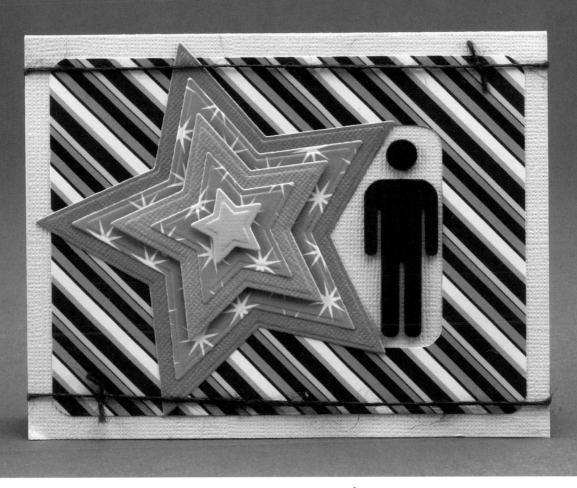

Super Dad Card

by Sarah Hodgkinson

Sarah layered nesting stars to create a large, simple embellishment for this card.

1 Fold a 5½" × 8½" (14cm × 21.5cm) piece of cream cardstock in half to create a standard 5½" × 4¼" (14cm × 10.75cm) card base.

2 Cut a piece of striped patterned paper to 5" × 3¾" (12.75cm × 9.5cm). Round the corners of the paper. Handcut a frame for the chipboard man.

3 Punch or die cut stars from coordinating cardstock and patterned paper and adhere and layer them onto the card front.

4 Tie twine around the card.

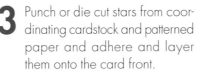

SUPPLIES

Cardstock (Core'dinations)
Patterned paper (Jillibean Soup)
Chipboard (Riff Raff Designs)
Twine (Jillibean Soup)
Dies (Spellbinders)
Ink (Tsukineko)
Punch (We R Memory Keepers)
Paper trimmer or scissors
Adhesive of choice

Father's Day Car Card

by Kimber McGray

In a rush to spend the day with Dad? Create a quick card using coordinating patterned papers and a die cut for a card that will drive home how much you care.

1 Fold a 5½" × 8½" (14cm × 21.5cm) piece of patterned paper in half to create a 5½" × 4¼" (14cm × 10.75cm) standard A2 card.

2 Cut a 1½" × 5½" (3.75cm × 14cm) piece of striped patterned paper and adhere it to the bottom front of the card.

3 Adhere the car die cut to the front of the card with foam adhesive.

4 Wrap tan twine around the card front 3 times and tie it into a small bow.

SUPPLIES

Patterned paper (My Mind's Eye)

Die cut (My Mind's Eye)

Twine (Jillibean Soup)

Paper trimmer or scissors

Adhesive of choice

Foam adhesive

Three Monsters Halloween Card

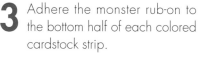

by Vivian Masket

Vivian used up scraps of cardstock to create this simple but humorous Halloween card.

1 Create the card base by folding an 8½" × 5½" (21.5 × 14cm) piece of black cardstock in half.

2 Cut three 1½" × 3¾" (3.75cm × 9.5cm) pieces of colored cardstock: one purple, one green, and one orange.

3 Adhere the monster rub-on to the bottom half of each colored cardstock strip.

4 Place a mini brad at the top of each colored cardstock strip.

5 Adhere the cardstock strips to the card front with foam adhesive.

SUPPLIES

Cardstock (Bazzill Basics)
Rub-ons (October Afternoon)
Brads (American Crafts)
Paper trimmer or scissors
Adhesive of choice
Foam adhesive

Have a Spooktacular Halloween! Card

by Laura Vegas

Laura used repetitive circular pieces on her card to create a lot of movement. The little ghosts add the Halloween feel.

1 Fold a 5½" × 8½" (14cm × 21.5cm) piece of patterned paper in half to create a standard 5½" × 4¼" (14cm × 10.75cm) card base.

2 Cut 3 circles out of black patterned paper measuring 4" (10.25cm), 2" (5cm) and 1¼" (3.25cm). Layer them on the card front and trim away the excess. Adhere them to the front of the card.

3 Embellish the card with stickers, buttons and tags.

SUPPLIES

Patterned paper (Jillibean Soup, Making Memories)

Stickers (Making Memories)

Buttons (Autumn Leaves by Creativity Inc.)

Tags (Making Memories)

Paper trimmer or scissors

Adhesive of choice

Simply Grateful Thanksgiving Card

by Kimber McGray

The colors of fall and a fabric brad with a woven pumpkin image
wish your loved ones a happy thanksgiving.

1 Fold an 8" × 4¼" (20.5cm × 10.75cm) piece of striped patterned paper in half to create a 4" × 4¼" (10.25cm × 10.75cm) card base.

2 Round the bottom corners of the card.

3 Die cut a piece of cream cardstock and stamp the image onto it.

4 Fold a ½" × 2" (1.25cm × 5cm) piece of floral patterned paper to create a loop and attach it to the die cut with a brad. Adhere it to the front of the card with foam adhesive.

SUPPLIES

Cardstock (Core'dinations)

Patterned paper (Making Memories)

Die (Spellbinders)

Brad (K&Company)

Stamps (Papertrey Ink)

Punch (We R Memory Keepers)

Paper trimmer or scissors

Foam adhesive

Mother's Day Bulletin Board

by Kimber McGray

Using a pre-made frame and bulletin board plus left over scraps from your card, you can create a quick gift for your mom that she can use all year long.

Supplies:

Frame board (Michaels); patterned paper (SEI); die cuts (K&Company); buttons (Stampin' Up!); thumb tacks (office supply store)

Halloween Candy Suckers

by Kimber McGray

When you need to "treat" a classroom full of "ghouls and goblins," quickly embellish some bulk suckers for a spooktacular treat.

Supplies:

Stickers (Making Memories); ribbon (Stampin' Up!); suckers (variety store)

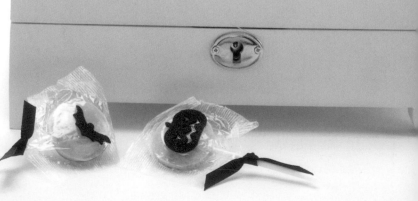

Elegant Valentine
by Linda Beeson

Supplies:

Cardstock (Core'dinations); punch (EK Success); embossing plate (Spellbinders); die (Spellbinders); brad (K&Company)

Glitter Hearts Card
by Stacy Cohen

Supplies:

Cardstock (Bazzill Basics); patterned papers (K&Company, me and my BIG ideas); chipboard (Melissa Frances, Heidi Swapp); gemstones (Kaisercraft); ribbon (Michaels); glitter (Marcella by K); punch (Martha Stewart Crafts); ink (ColorBox by Clearsnap); lace

Circles of Love
by Kristie Larsen

Supplies:

Cardstock (Papertrey Ink); button (Papertrey Ink); ribbon (American Crafts); punches (Stampin' Up!, Marvy, Fiskars)

Vintage Valentine's Day Card
by Stacy Cohen

Supplies:

Cardstock (Bazzill Basics); patterned paper (Graphic 45); chipboard (Tattered Angels); pin (Maya Road); ribbon (Details by Making memories); rub-on (Marcella by K); ink (ColorBox by Clearsnap); vintage lace and vintage glitter glass

Lots of Love Card
by Paula Gilarde

Love Has Wings Card
by Fabrè Sanders

Puppy Love Card
by Barb Wong

Supplies:

Cardstock (Core'dinations); patterned paper (SEI); chipboard (Making Memories); punch (Stampin' Up!); embossing folder (Provo Craft Cuttlebug); ink (Maya Road); punch (EK Success)

Supplies:

Cardstock (Wausau Paper); patterned paper (Luxe Designs); stamp (Luxe Designs); ink (Stampin' Up!, ColorBox by Clearsnap); marker (Stampin' Up!)

Supplies:

Cardstock (Bazzill Basics); patterned paper (Jillibean Soup); chipboard (Making Memories); stamp (Purple Onion Designs); decorative scissors (Fiskars); ink (StazOn by Tsukineko)

Witch on Broom Halloween Card
by Jennifer Buck

Flying Witch Card
by Kimber McGray

Supplies:

Cardstock (Papertrey Ink); patterned paper (Stampin' Up!); stamp (Papertrey Ink); gems (Papertrey Ink); ribbon (Martha Stewart Crafts); ink (Papertrey Ink)

Supplies:

Patterned paper (BoBunny Press, Making Memories); stickers (Making Memories); punches (Marvy, Fiskars); twine (Jillibean Soup); ink (ColorBox by Clearsnap)

Bubbling Caldron Card
by Kimber McGray

Spider Halloween Card
by Kim Moreno

Go Batty! Card
by Kandis Smith

Supplies:

Cardstock (Core'dinations); patterned paper (Doodlebug Design); stickers (Doodlebug Design); ribbon (Doodlebug Design); punch (Stampin' Up!); embossing folder (Provo Craft Cuttlebug)

Supplies:

Cardstock (Core'dinations); patterned papers (Glitz Design); ribbon (Close to My Heart); gemstones (Kaisercraft); tool (Scor-Pal); punches (Creative Memories, EK Success); miscellaneous spider

Supplies:

Cardstock (Doodlebug Design); patterned paper (Doodlebug Design); ribbon (Doodlebug Design); brads (Doodlebug Design); gemstones (Doodlebug Design); stamp (Hero Arts); colored pencils (Prismacolor); buttons (Dress It Up! by Jesse James Beads)

Fall Pumpkin Card
by Allison Cope

Give Thanks Card
by Sarah Hodgkinson

Supplies:

Cardstock (Bazzill Basics); stamps (Papertrey Ink); patterned papers (My Mind's Eye); ink (Ranger Industries); die (Spellbinders); ribbon (Stampin' Up!); die cut (My Mind's Eye); punch (MarthaStewart Crafts)

Supplies:

Cardstock (Core'dinations); ribbon (American Crafts); buttons (Jillibean Soup); twine (Jillibean Soup); punch (We R Memory Keepers)

A Little Bit of Luck in Your Corner Card
by Kimber McGray

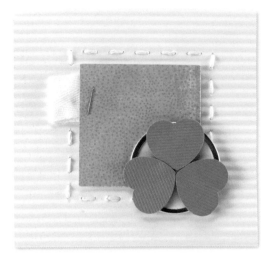

See page 123 for a basic sketch of this card.

Supplies:

Cardstock (Papertrey Ink, Bazzill Basics); patterned paper (Crate Paper); punch (Creative Memories); paper crimper (Fiskars); embroidery floss (DMC); twill (Wrights); tag (office supply store)

Triple the Luck Card
by Kimber McGray

Supplies:

Cardstock (Jillibean Soup); patterned paper (Jillibean Soup, BoBunny Press); inchies (Inchie Arts); stamps (Hero Arts); button (Jillibean Soup); ribbon (BasicGrey); ink (Stampin' Up!); punch (Stampin' Up!, We R Memory Keepers)

Chocolate Bunny Card
by Kimber McGray

Supplies:

Cardstock (Jillibean Soup, Core'dinations); patterned paper (October Afternoon, BoBunny Press); die cut (October Afternoon, Provo Craft Cricut); ink (Close to My Heart); punch (Fiskars)

Floral Wreath and Cross Easter Card
by Kimber McGray

Supplies:

Cardstock (Core'dinations); patterned paper (BasicGrey); stamp (Unity Stamp Company); ink (Close to My Heart); marker (Copic); ribbon (Creative Impressions); gemstones (Zva Creative)

Peace Easter Card
by Kimber McGray

Supplies:

Cardstock (Core'dinations); patterned paper (BasicGrey); sticker (BasicGrey); stamp (Unity Stamp Company); ink (Memento by Tsukineko, BasicGrey); clip (Stampin' Up!); gemstone (Zva Creative); ribbon (Creative Impressions)

Mother's Day Flower Pot
by Kandi Phillips

Sewing Machine Mother's Day Card
by Laura O'Donnell

Supplies:

Cardstock (Stampin' Up!); patterned paper (Scenic Route Paper Co.); punch (Stampin' Up!); ribbon (Stampin' UP!); flowers (Stampin' Up!, American Crafts); buttons (Stampin' Up!)

Supplies:

Cardstock (Bazzill Basics, Cornish Heritage Farms); stamps (Cornish Heritage Farms); ink (Moment by Tsukineko); die (Spellbinders); paper flowers (Prima Marketing, Inc.)

Father's Day Shirt and Tie Card
by Kimber McGray

Golf Ball on Tee Father's Day Card
by Kimber McGray

Retro BBQ Father's Day Card
by Kimber McGray

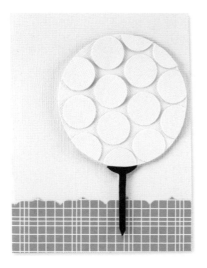

See page 123 for a basic sketch of this card.

Supplies:

Patterned paper (Jillibean Soup, Scenic Route Paper Co.)

Supplies:

Cardstock (Core'dinations); patterned paper (Jillibean Soup); punches (Fiskars, EK Success)

Supplies:

Cardstock (Core'dinations); patterned paper (BasicGrey); punch (Stampin' Up!); ribbon (Stampin' Up!); stamp (Unity Stamp Company); ink (Memento by Tsukineko)

Special Day

Weddings, anniversaries, births, baby showers and bridal showers are monumental events in our lives. Welcome a new baby into the world, wish a bride and groom a happy life together and celebrate years of wedded bliss. Don't forget to say congratulations to a special graduate. Custom make a card to recognize these wonderful events.

Baby Shower Card

by Kimber McGray

A circle punch and some buttons from your craft box help create this sweet baby shower card in a jiffy.

1 Fold a 5½" × 8½" (14cm × 21.5cm) piece of yellow cardstock in half to create a 5½" × 4¼" (14cm × 10.75cm) standard A2 card.

2 Trim a prescalloped piece of white cardstock to 4" (10.25cm) wide. Run the white cardstock through the embossing machine with a Swiss Dot embossing folder to create the embossing down the middle of the white cardstock.

3 Machine stitch around the perimeter of the embossed dots and adhere the white cardstock to the front of the yellow card base.

4 To create the baby carriage, punch a 3" (7.5cm) circle from yellow patterned paper. Cut out a 1½" (3.75cm) square from the right corner of the circle. Add a scalloped piece of white cardstock to the top edge of the baby carriage. Tie a white ribbon around the carriage and tie it into a bow. Adhere the baby carriage to the front of the card with foam adhesive.

5 Add 2 buttons to the bottom of the circle for baby carriage wheels.

SUPPLIES

Cardstock (Bazzill Basics)
Patterned paper (Imaginisce)
Ribbon (Creative Impressions)
Buttons (Stampin' Up!)
Punch (Marvy, Stampin' Up!)
Embossing folder (Provo Craft Cuttlebug)
Embroidery floss (DMC)
Paper trimmer or scissors
Adhesive of choice
Foam adhesive
Sewing machine

See the Dry Embossing technique on page 15 to learn how to achieve this textured background.

Big Brother/Big Sister Cards

by Vivian Masket

Don't forget about the new big brother or new big sister on the day the baby joins the family. Vivian created this great set of cards that a proud new sibling would love to receive.

1 Create the card base by folding an 8½" × 5½" (21.5cm × 14cm) piece of white cardstock in half.

2 Cut a 4¼" × 5½" (10.75cm × 14cm) piece of alphabet patterned paper and adhere it to the card base.

3 Cut or punch a 3½" (9cm) square postage stamp frame from black cardstock.

4 Adhere a damask patterned sticker to coordinating cardstock, and trim to 3¼" (8.25cm) square.

5 Adhere the frame to the damask square.

6 Apply the rub-ons to the front of the framed square.

7 Tie a bow in the center of a 10" (25.5cm) length of ribbon.

8 Attach a brad through the center of the bow.

9 Adhere the ends of the bow to the top of the framed square.

10 Attach the ribbon and the square frame to the front of the card.

SUPPLIES

Cardstock (Bazzill Basics)

Patterned paper (KI Memories)

Stickers (Heidi Swapp)

Rub-ons (October Afternoon)

Brads (American Crafts)

Die-cutting machine (Making Memories Slice)

Paper trimmer or scissors

Adhesive of choice

Welcome Little One Card

by Lynn Ghahary

Mixing pinks, blues and yellows make this baby card perfect for
any little one you wish to welcome into the world.

1 Fold a 5½" × 8½" (14cm × 21.5cm) piece of yellow cardstock in half to create a 5½" × 4¼" (14cm × 10.75cm) standard card base. Round the upper corners of the card.

2 Cut a 5¼" × 1½" (13.25cm × 3.75cm) piece of blue patterned paper. Round the edges and adhere them to the front of the card.

3 Cut a 1" × 5½" (2.5cm × 14cm) piece of striped patterned paper and adhere it to the card front.

4 Cut a 1½" × 5½" (3.75cm × 14cm) piece of theme patterned paper and adhere it to the front of the card. Machine stitch along the seam of the striped and theme papers.

5 Add a ¼" × 5½" (6mm × 14cm) piece of white cardstock that has been punched with a decorative border punch to the front of the card.

6 Tie a yellow ribbon around the front of the card and embellish it with a button and stickpins.

SUPPLIES

Cardstock (Bazzill Basics)

Patterned paper (October Afternoon)

Ribbon (Wrights)

Tags (KI Memories)

Pins (Fancy Pants Designs)

Punches (Stampin' Up!, EK Success)

Paper trimmer or scissors

Adhesive of choice

Sewing machine

Pink Gift Card Holder

by Sherry Wright

Simple folds create a great gift card enclosure. Tuck a gift card inside for the mom-to-be or bride-to-be.

1 Cut a 6" × 12" (15.25cm × 30.5cm) piece of pink patterned paper.

2 Score the paper at 3" (7.5cm), 6" (15.25cm) and 9" (22.75cm) to create a 4 panel card.

3 Slice the paper at the 6" (15.25cm) score mark, leaving at least 1" (2.5cm) at the top and bottom of the fold.

4 Place adhesive along 3 sides of one of the center panels. Do not place adhesive along the side with the slit.

5 Adhere the middle 2 panels together by folding the 6" × 12" (15.25cm × 30.5cm) paper in half along the center fold.

6 Punch a half circle out of the center fold with the slit. This is where the gift card will slide into the card.

7 Embellish the front of the card with ribbon. Slide the straight pins into the knot of the ribbon.

SUPPLIES

Cardstock (Prism Papers)
Patterned paper (Dream Street)
Ribbon (Berwick Offray)
Punch (McGill)
Tool (Scor-Pal)
Pins
Paper trimmer or scissors
Adhesive of choice

See Gift Card Holder on page 18 to see photos for this great gift-giving technique.

Always and Forever Wedding Card

by Laura Vegas

A perfect marriage of contemporary and traditional style: a modern color combination mixes with traditional tulle and pearl stickpins.

1 Fold a 5½" × 8½" (14cm × 21.5cm) piece of white cardstock in half to create a standard 5½" × 4¼" (14cm × 10.75cm) card base.

2 Cut a 2½" × 5½" (6.25cm × 14cm) piece of black patterned paper and adhere it to the front of the card.

3 Cut a 1¾" × 5½" (4.5cm × 14cm) piece of grey patterned paper and adhere it to the front of the card. Round the corners.

4 Cut a 2" × 2¼" (5cm × 5.75cm) piece of white cardstock, round the corners and adhere it to the front of the card.

5 Layer the flowers and brad and attach them to the front of the card.

6 Slide 2 pearl stickpins into a strip of ribbon and adhere the ribbon to the front of the card.

SUPPLIES

Cardstock (American Crafts)

Patterned paper (Making Memories)

Ribbon (American Crafts)

Flowers (Making Memories)

Pins (Making Memories)

Brads (Making Memories)

Punch (Creative Memories)

Paper trimmer or scissors

Adhesive of choice

Wedding Cake Card

by Kimber McGray

What bride doesn't love Tiffany Blue and cake? Take cues from wedding traditions to add sentimental touches to your card.

1 Fold a 5½" × 8½" (14cm × 21.5cm) piece of white cardstock in half to create a 5½" × 4¼" (14cm × 10.75cm) standard A2 card.

2 Cut a 3¼" × 4" (8.25cm × 10.25cm) piece of blue cardstock and adhere it to the right side of the card front, leaving a ⅛" (3mm) border around the edges.

3 Cut a 2¼" × 4" (5.75cm × 10.25cm) piece of striped patterned paper and adhere it to the left side of the card front, leaving a ⅛" (3mm) border around the edges.

4 Layer and adhere a 4¼" × 1" (10.75cm × 2.5cm) piece of die-cut cardstock over the seam.

5 Tie a bow in a piece of blue ribbon, and attach it to the front. Wrap the top end of the ribbon around the back and the bottom end around to the inside of the card, and attach both ends.

6 Add a premade, dimensional cake embellishment to the blue cardstock.

SUPPLIES

Cardstock (Papertrey Ink, Stampin' Up!)

Patterned paper (Making Memories)

Die-cut cardstock (Making Memories)

Ribbon (Papertrey Ink)

Dimensional sticker (Jolee's Boutique)

Paper trimmer or scissors

Adhesive of choice

See page 122 for a basic sketch of this card.

Patchwork Heart Card

by Kandis Smith

Pull at their heartstrings with a paper patchwork card created with love.

1 Fold a 12" × 4½" (30.5cm × 11.5cm) piece of green cardstock in half to create a 6" × 4½" (15.25cm × 11.5cm) card base.

2 Emboss the front of the card and lightly sand the embossed pattern.

3 Cut four 2" (5cm) squares from coordinating patterned paper, adhere them to the front of the card and machine stitch around the borders of each square.

4 Tie twine around the front of the card and tie it into a bow. Embellish with a brad.

5 Adhere a die-cut label to the front of the card with foam adhesive.

6 Stamp the heart image onto a scrap of white cardstock. Cut out the image and adhere it to the front of the card with foam adhesive.

7 Stamp 2 little heart images onto the lower corner of the patchwork square.

SUPPLIES

Cardstock (Core'dinations)

Patterned paper (October Afternoon)

Twine (Jillibean Soup)

Button (Dress It Up by Jesse James Beads)

Tag (October Afternoon)

Embossing folder (Provo Craft Cuttlebug)

Stamps (Hero Arts)

Ink (Ranger Industries)

Paper trimmer or scissors

Adhesive of choice

Foam adhesive

Sandpaper

Sewing machine

Elegant Wedding Card

by Allison Cope

Allison creates a beautiful and elegant wedding card by adding white embossed stamped flowers to the front of a black card base and adding a touch of whimsy with a tulle butterfly.

1 Fold a 5½" × 8½" (14cm × 21.5cm) piece of black cardstock in half to create a standard 4¼" × 5½" (10.75cm × 14cm) card base.

2 Stamp the images with watermark ink and cover them with embossing powder. Shake off the excess powder and heat to melt the powder.

3 Die cut the butterfly from black cardstock, white cardstock and tulle. Layer the pieces together and embellish the butterfly with silver gemstones.

4 Die cut a white cardstock label and embellish it with silver gemstones. Adhere it to the front of the card.

See Heat Embossing on page 14 to see this embellishing technique in action.

S U P P L I E S

Cardstock (Bazzill Basics, Prism Papers)

Stamps (Papertrey Ink)

Embossing powder (Hero Arts)

Watermark ink (VersaMark by Tsukineko)

Gemstones (Michaels)

Die (Spellbinders)

Tulle (Bazzill Basics)

Heat gun

Adhesive of choice

Wedding Shower Card

by Kimber McGray

A fun take on the "shower" theme uses chipboard umbrellas to dress up a card for the bride-to-be.

1 Fold a 5½" × 8½" (14cm × 21.5cm) piece of yellow patterned paper in half to create a standard 5½" × 4¼" (14cm × 10.75cm) card base.

2 Cut a 4½" × 4¼" (11.5cm × 10.75cm) piece of blue patterned paper and adhere it to the top of the card base.

3 Scallop punch a 4¼" × ½" (10.75cm × 1.25cm) piece of matching blue patterned paper and add it to the card front.

4 Tie a blue ribbon around the front of the card.

5 Adhere chipboard embellishments to the front of the card.

6 Outline the border of the card with a white gel pen.

7 Round the bottom corners of the card.

SUPPLIES

Patterned paper (American Crafts)

Chipboard (American Crafts)

Ribbon (American Crafts)

Punch (Stampin' Up!, We R Memory Keepers)

Pen (Uni-ball Signo)

Paper trimmer or scissors

Adhesive of choice

Elegant Anniversary Card

by Jennifer Buck

Treat your sweetie with this anniversary card that features a delicious looking chocolate cake topped with your heart.

1 Fold a 4¼" × 11" (10.75cm × 28cm) piece of gold cardstock in half to create a standard 4¼" × 5½" (10.75cm × 14cm) card base.

2 Cut a 4¼" × 4" (10.75cm × 10.25cm) piece of red cardstock and adhere it to the front of the card.

3 Cut a 3¾" × 4¼" (9.5cm × 10.75cm) piece of red patterned paper and adhere it to the front of the card.

4 Emboss a 1¾" × 4¼" (4.5cm × 10.75cm) piece of red cardstock and adhere it to the front of the card.

5 Stamp the cake image on a piece of white cardstock, layer it onto a piece of red cardstock and adhere this to the front of the card with foam adhesive.

6 Stamp the image again onto a piece of white cardstock. Color the image with markers, cut it out and adhere it to the front of the card with foam adhesive.

7 Tie a ribbon around the front of the card.

SUPPLIES

Cardstock (Bazzill Basics, Papertrey Ink)

Patterned paper (Papertrey Ink)

Ribbon (Papertrey Ink)

Stamp (Unity Stamp Company)

Markers (Copic)

Embossing folder (Provo Craft Cuttlebug)

Ink (Papertrey Ink)

Paper trimmer or scissors

Adhesive of choice

Foam adhesive

We're Quite a Pair/Pear Card

by Kelly Goree

Kelly uses a set of pears to wish a pair of friends a happy anniversary.

1 Fold a 10" × 5" (25.5cm × 12.75cm) piece of olive cardstock in half to create a square 5" × 5" (12.75cm × 12.75cm) card base.

2 Cover the front of the card with a 5" × 5" (12.75cm × 12.75cm) blue piece of patterned paper. Round the bottom corners of the card.

3 Cut a 4" × 5" (10.25cm × 12.75cm) piece of brown patterned paper and adhere it to the front of the card.

4 Cut a 1¾" × 5" (4.5cm × 12.75cm) piece of olive patterned paper and adhere it to the front of the card.

5 Add a 5" × ½" (12.75cm × 1.25cm) strip of white cardstock that has been punched with a decorative edge punch to the front of the card.

6 Wrap a piece of twine around the card front and tie it into a knot.

7 Cover a chipboard piece with white cardstock and trim off the excess with a craft knife, ink the edges and adhere it to the front of the card with foam adhesive.

8 Embellish the front of the card with chipboard pieces and faux stitching.

SUPPLIES

Cardstock (Bazzill Basics)

Patterned paper (BasicGrey)

Chipboard (BasicGrey, Pink Paislee)

Ink (ColorBox by Clearsnap)

Punches (Fiskars)

Pen

Paper trimmer or scissors

Adhesive of choice

Foam adhesive

See Faux Stitching on page 12 to learn how to do this cute embellishment.

Elementary School Graduation Card

by Kim Moreno

Celebrate the accomplishments of a young student with a graduation card made just for them.

1 Fold an 8" × 5" (20.5cm × 12.75cm) piece of red cardstock in half to create a 4" × 5" (10.25cm × 12.75cm) card base. Round the corners of the card.

2 Cut a 4½" × 3½" (11.5cm × 9cm) piece of theme patterned paper and use a decorative edge punch on the top and bottom edges. Adhere it to the front of the card.

3 Cut a 4" (10.25cm) star from a die or by hand. Ink the edges and adhere it to the front of the card.

4 Hand-draw a diploma inspired by the ribbon design, ink the edges and adhere it to the front of the card with foam adhesive.

5 Tie a piece of ribbon around the diploma and tie the ribbon into a bow. Embellish the card with a button and a stickpin.

6 Cut a small strip of striped patterned paper and attach it to the front of the card with 3 brads.

SUPPLIES

Cardstock (Core'dinations)
Patterned paper (Jillibean Soup)
Punch (Stampin' Up!)
Ribbon (Wal-Mart)
Brads (American Crafts)
Pin (Heidi Grace Designs)
Paper trimmer or scissors
Adhesive of choice
Foam adhesive

Anniversary/Wedding Gift Box

by Lisa Dorsey

Good things come in small packages. This elegant gift box is the perfect vessel for a meaningful gift for the newlyweds or a couple celebrating their 40th anniversary.

Supplies:

Cardstock (Bazzill Basics); patterned papers (GCD Studios, BoBunny Press, Making Memories); chipboard (Heidi Swapp); ribbon (Michaels); button (Jesse James Beads); punch (EK Success); ink (ColorBox by Clearsnap); twine (May Arts); box (Expo International)

Baby Shower Gift Bag

by Kimber McGray

Using the same items and techniques as you did for your Baby Shower Card (page 84), make a few adjustments for a great coordinating gift bag.

Supplies:

Bag (Creative Café by Creative Imaginations); patterned paper (Imaginisce); buttons (Stampin' Up!, Fancy Pants Designs); ribbon (Creative Impressions); punch (Stampin' Up!); clip (Making Memories)

New Baby Love Card
by Carolyn King

Supplies:

Cardstock (Gina K Designs); patterned paper (My Mind's Eye); die cuts (Anna Griffin); stamps (Gina K Designs); ink (Memento by Tsukineko); markers (Copic); ribbon (Berwick Offray); punch (Creative Memories)

White Dove Baptism Card
by Kimber McGray

Supplies:

Cardstock (Papertrey Ink, Jillibean Soup); stamp (Stampin' Up!); ink (Jo-Ann Craft Essentials); ribbon (Creative Impressions); pins (Fancy Pants Designs); gemstones (Zva Creative); embossing folder (Provo Craft Cuttlebug)

Welcome Baby Card
by Sarah Hodgkinson

Supplies:

Cardstock (Core'dinations, Jillibean Soup); patterned paper (Scenic Route); stamps (Hero Arts); rub-on (Heidi Grace Designs); ink (Tsukineko)

Baby Girl Card
by Summer Fullerton

Supplies:

Cardstock (Bazzill Basics); patterned paper (October Afternoon); die cuts (October Afternoon); brads (BasicGrey); punch (EK Success)

Chicks in a Row Baby Card
by Tina Fussell

Supplies:

Cardstock (Papertrey Ink); patterned paper (Papertrey Ink); stamps (Papertrey Ink); ink (VersaMark by Tsukineko, Papertrey Ink); embossing powder (Stampin' Up!); twine

Baby Boy One Piece Card
by Paula Gilarde

Supplies:

Cardstock (Core'dinations); patterned paper (SEI); chipboard (Die Cuts With a View); punches (EK Success)

Baby Girl Giraffe Card
by Kimber McGray

See page 123 for a basic sketch of this card.

Supplies:

Cardstock (Core'dinations); patterned paper (BoBunny Press, Making Memories); sticker (Making Memories); embossing folder (Provo Craft Cuttlebug); punches (We R Memory Keepers, Stampin' Up!)

Baby Girl One Piece Card
by Jeanne Streiff

Supplies:

Cardstock (Prism Papers); stamps (Hanna Stamps); markers (Copic); sprinkles (Flower Soft); ink (Ranger Industries); button

Baby Boy Booties Card
by Terri Hayes

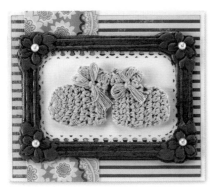

Supplies:

Cardstock (Bazzill Basics); patterned paper (Anna Griffin, Making Memories); chipboard (Making Memories); crocheted booties (Anna Griffin); gemstones (Kaisercraft); punch (Martha Stewart)

Momma Duck and Ducklings Baby Card
by Debbie Standard

Supplies:

Cardstock (Core'dinations); patterned paper (October Afternoon); punch (Fiskars)

Baby Girl Clothesline Card
by Kimber McGray

Supplies:

Cardstock (Core'dinations); patterned paper (BoBunny Press); stickers (K&Company); gemstones (Zva Creative), punch (Stampin' Up!)

Shining Stars Baby Boy Card
by Kimber McGray

See page 123 for a basic sketch of this card.

Supplies:

Cardstock (Core'dinations, Bazzill Basics); stickers (Making Memories); buttons (Making Memories); brads (Doodlebug Design); embossing folder (Provo Craft Cuttlebug); embroidery floss (DMC); pen (Uni-ball Signo)

Baby Paper-Pieced Quilt Card
by Kimber McGray

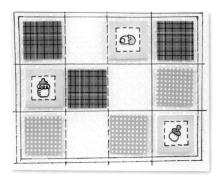

Supplies:

Cardstock (Papertrey Ink); patterned paper (Jillibean Soup, American Crafts); inchies (Inchie Arts); stamps (Doodlebug Design); ink (Memento by Tsukineko); markers (Copic); colored pencils (Prismacolor); embossing folder (Provo Craft Cuttlebug)

Stitched Cross Baptism Card
by Kimber McGray

Supplies:

Cardstock (Papertrey Ink, Core'dinations); stamp (Stampin' Up!); patterned paper (Making Memories); ink (Stampin' Up!); punch (Marvy); gemstones (Zva Creative)

Wedding Cupcake Card
by Laura O'Donnell

Supplies:

Cardstock (Neenah, American Crafts); patterned papers (Jenni Bowlin Studio); stamps (Pink Persimmon); ink (Memento by Tsukineko); markers (Copic)

Wedding Shower Card
by Kimber McGray

Supplies:

Cardstock (Papertrey Ink); patterned paper (Making Memories); embossing folder (Provo Craft Cuttlebug); stickers (Jolee's Boutique); ribbon (Papertrey Ink)

Bride Silhouette Card
by Charity Hassel

Supplies:

Cardstock (Core'dinations); patterned papers (Piggy Tales); gemstones (Zva Creative); flowers (Maya Road); templates (Scotch/3M); vellum

Bride and Groom Card
by Cathy Schellenberg

Supplies:

Cardstock (Stampin' Up!); patterned paper (Sharon Ann Collection); flowers (Prima Marketing, Inc.); glitter glue (Ranger Industries); ink (StazOn by Tsukineko); stamp (DeNami Design); punch (EK Success); lace; stamp board

25th Anniversary Card
by Kimber McGray

Supplies:

Cardstock (Core'dinations); patterned paper (Making Memories); chipboard (BasicGrey); ink (Brilliance by Tsukineko); gemstones (Zva Creative)

50th Anniversary Card
by Kimber McGray

Supplies:

Patterned paper (SEI); die cut (SEI); chipboard (BasicGrey); rub-on (Jenni Bowlin Studio); ribbon (Creative Impressions); ink (Brilliance by Tsukineko)

Proud as a Peacock
Kindergarten Graduation Card
by Kimber McGray

Supplies:

Cardstock (Core'dinations); patterned paper (Crate Paper, Autumn Leaves by Creativity, Inc.); sticker (Doodlebug Design); ribbon (Jillibean Soup); punch (Stampin' Up!); stamp (Inkadinkado); ink (Memento by Tsukineko)

Tassel Graduation Card
by Kimber McGray

Supplies:

Cardstock (Papertrey Ink); numbers (American Crafts); eyelet (We R Memory Keepers); punches (We R Memory Keepers, Stampin' Up!); embroidery floss (DMC); embossing folder (Provo Craft Cuttlebug)

Black-and-White
Graduation Card
by Ellen Sosnoski

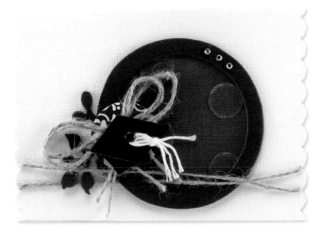

Supplies:

Cardstock (Core'dinations); patterned paper (American Crafts); chipboard (Cosmo Cricket); twine (Jillibean Soup); sticker (Jolee's Boutique); gemstones (Queen & Co.); punches (Stampin' Up!, Creative Memories)

Star Graduation Card
by Kimber McGray

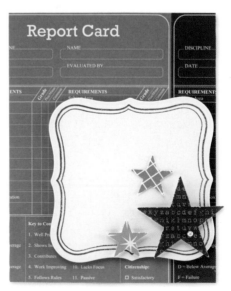

Supplies:

Cardstock (Papertrey Ink); patterned paper (Jillibean Soup); stamps (Papertrey Ink); ink (Close to My Heart); dies (Spellbinders); gemstones (Zva Creative)

CHAPTER

5

Sweet Sentiments

Simple cards to keep in touch are some of the best ones to receive. Whether you are simply thinking of a friend, missing them or wanting to say "Hi," a card with a simple design can be used for many occasions.

New Home Birdie Card

by Kimber McGray

The whimsical touch of using a birdhouse and birdies makes this a fun card to give to a friend who just bought their first home or to a new neighbor who just moved in next door.

1 Fold a 5½" × 8½" (14cm × 21.5cm) piece of tan cardstock in half to create a 5½" × 4¼" (14cm × 10.75cm) standard A2 card.

2 Cut a piece of red patterned paper to 3¼" × 5½" (8.25cm × 14cm) and create a scalloped edge with a scallop border punch on one end. Adhere it to the front of the card. Add machine stitching along the top.

3 Tie a white ribbon around the birdhouse die cut and add a button to the center of the bow with a piece of thin twine. Adhere the birdhouse and birds to the front of the card with foam adhesive.

SUPPLIES

Cardstock (Core'dinations)
Patterned paper (Crate Paper)
Die cuts (Crate Paper)
Ribbon (Creative Impressions)
Button (Stampin' Up!)
Punch (Stampin' Up!)
Twine
Paper trimmer or scissors
Adhesive of choice
Foam adhesive
Sewing machine

We're Moving/We've Moved Card

by Kimber McGray

Wouldn't it be nice to just pick up your house and all its belongings when you move? This card can be made by the dozen to let your friends and family know you have moved.

1 Cut a piece of kraft cardstock to 7" × 8½" (17.75cm × 21.5cm) and fold in half to create a 7" × 4¼" (17.75cm × 10.75cm) card. This will fit in an A7 envelope.

2 Cut a piece of cloud patterned paper to 2¾" × 6¾" (7cm × 17cm). Adhere it to the front of the card.

3 Cut a piece of striped patterned paper to 1¾" × 6¾" (4.5cm × 17cm) and adhere it to the front of the card.

4 Stamp a truck image on white cardstock, color it in with markers and adhere it to the front of the card.

5 Cover 4 chipboard house pieces with an ink that coordinates with your paper choices. Adhere the pieces to the front of the card: 3 of the houses grouped together and 1 on the back of the truck.

6 Wrap a long length of thin twine around the front of the card 3 times, and tie it into a bow.

SUPPLIES

Cardstock (Jillibean Soup)

Patterned paper (October Afternoon, Making Memories)

Chipboard (Maya Road)

Stamp (Unity Stamp Company)

Markers (Copic)

Ink (ColorBox by Clearsnap, Memento by Tsukineko)

Twine

Paper trimmer or scissors

Adhesive of choice

Missing You Leaf Card

by Kimber McGray

The gentle sweeping of the falling leaves and the colors of this card fit right
in with that feeling when you are missing a friend or loved one.

1 Fold a 10" × 7" (25.5cm × 17.75cm) piece of cream cardstock in half to create a 5" × 7" (12.75cm × 17.75cm) standard A7 card.

2 Cut 2 pieces of patterned paper to 4½" × 6½" (11.5cm × 16.5cm). Adhere the yellow patterned paper to the front of the card with a 1/8" (3mm) border all around.

3 Draw a sweeping curve onto the brown paper and cut it out with scissors. Adhere it on top of the yellow patterned paper. Machine stitch around the edge of the patterned papers.

4 Adhere 3 chipboard leaves along the curve of the brown patterned paper.

! **See page 122 for a basic sketch of this card.**

SUPPLIES

Cardstock (Core'dinations)

Patterned paper (SEI and Jillibean Soup)

Chipboard (Cosmo Cricket)

A Little Birdie Card

by Summer Fullerton

Send your favorite "chick" a little birdie card to brighten her day. She'll think you are so "tweet"!

1 Fold a 10" × 4¼" (25.5cm × 10.75cm) piece of olive cardstock in half to create a 5" × 4¼" (12.75cm × 10.75cm) card base.

2 Cut a piece of kraft patterned paper to 3¾" × 4¾" (9.5cm × 12cm) and adhere it to the front of the card.

3 Adhere the die-cut circle to the front of the card.

4 Attach yellow flowers to the front of the card with yellow brads.

5 Adhere the bird die cut to the front of the card with foam adhesive and tie a tag to the tail. Embellish it with a gemstone eye.

SUPPLIES

Cardstock (Bazzill Basics)

Patterned paper (Jillibean Soup)

Die cut (Jillibean Soup, My Mind's Eye, Creative Imaginations)

Twine (Jillibean Soup)

Flowers (Prima Marketing, Inc.)

Brads (BasicGrey)

Gemstone (Kaisercraft)

Paper trimmer or scissors

Adhesive of choice

Pink Flower Card

by Kim Moreno

Send this card to your girliest of girlfriends. Kim decked her card out
with lots of scallops and gemstones for a friend with style.

1 Fold an 8½" × 4¾" (21.5cm × 12cm) piece of pink cardstock in half to create a 4¼" × 4¾" (10.75cm × 12cm) card base.

2 Score lines along the front of the card base and sand it gently to show the core.

3 Cut a piece of pink patterned paper to 2" × 4¾" (5cm × 12cm) and adhere it to the front of the card.

4 Create a decorative scalloped edge with a punch on a piece of 4¾" × ½" (12cm × 1.25cm) floral patterned paper. Adhere the scalloped paper to the front of the card.

5 Emboss a ½" × 4¾" (1.25cm × 12cm) piece of pink cardstock, gently sand the embossing and adhere it to the front of the card.

6 Adhere a die-cut scallop strip to the top of the card, punch notches in the card front and tie with string.

7 Punch 2 flowers from coordinating floral patterned paper, adhere them to the card front and embellish with gemstones.

SUPPLIES

Cardstock (Core'dinations)

Patterned papers (Dream Street)

Die cut (Doodlebug Design)

Gemstones (Glitz Design)

Punch (EK Success, Martha Stewart Crafts)

Embossing folder (Provo Craft Cuttlebug)

Scoring tool (Scor-Pal)

Paper trimmer or scissors

Adhesive of choice

Flying By to Say "Hi" Butterfly Card

by Melissa Phillips

Butterflies are such an inspiring sight. Sending a butterfly-embellished card to a friend will sure bring a smile to her face.

1 Fold a 7" × 5" (17.75cm × 12.75cm) piece of cream cardstock in half to create a 3½" × 5" (9cm × 12.75cm) card base.

2 Cut a 3¼" × 4¾" (8.25cm × 12cm) piece of yellow patterned paper and ink the edges with chalk ink. Adhere the paper to the front of the card.

3 Cut 4 strips of coordinating patterned paper to 2¾" × 4¼" (7cm × 10.75cm). Ink all the edges and adhere them to the front of the card. Machine stitch along the edges.

5 Tie a bow in a piece of pink ribbon, and attach it to the front. Wrap the top end of the ribbon around the back and the bottom end around to the inside of the card, and attach both ends.

6 Embellish the card with gemstones and a die-cut butterfly.

 See Inking Edges on page 17 to learn about this textural technique.

SUPPLIES

Cardstock (Papertrey Ink)

Patterned paper (BasicGrey)

Stamps (Papertrey Ink)

Ribbon (Papertrey Ink)

Buttons (Papertrey Ink)

Gemstones (Zva Creative)

Ink (Ranger Industries, Papertrey Ink)

Die cut (K&Company)

Paper trimmer or scissors

Adhesive of choice

Sewing machine

109

Singing Bird Card

by Vivian Masket

Sing the praises of your friendship by sending this cheery card to a friend.

1 Create the card base by folding an 8½" × 5½" (21.5cm × 14cm) piece of cardstock in half.

2 Cut a 4¼" × 5½" (10.75cm × 14cm) piece of sheet music patterned paper and adhere it to the front of the card.

3 Cut a 2½" × 5½" (6.25cm × 14cm) piece of pink patterned paper. Tear the right-hand long edge and adhere the paper to the front of the card.

4 Machine stitch wavy lines along the pink patterned paper to create the illusion of movement.

5 Print out a 1¼" (3.25cm) tall musical note clip art image template, place it on the black cardstock and cut out the image. Adhere it to the front of the card with foam adhesive.

6 Adhere the bird die cut to the front of the card with foam adhesive.

SUPPLIES

Cardstock (Bazzill Basics)
Patterned paper (October Afternoon)
Die cut (October Afternoon)
Clip art (Microsoft Word)
Paper trimmer or scissors
Adhesive of choice
Foam adhesive
Sewing machine

Friends Silhouette Card

by Paula Gilarde

The sweet image of the friends holding hands is perfect for young friends to send to each other.

1 Fold a 5½" × 8½" (14cm × 21.5cm) piece of cream cardstock in half to create a standard 5½" × 4¼" (14cm × 10.75cm) card base.

2 Punch the bottom front edge of the card with a border punch.

3 Line the inside of the card front with a 4¼" × 5½" (10.75cm × 14cm) piece of floral patterned paper.

4 Tie a ribbon around the front of the card.

5 Adhere 2 girl image punches to the front of the card.

6 Adhere the chipboard circle to the front of the card.

SUPPLIES

Cardstock (Core'dinations)
Patterned paper (Cosmo Cricket)
Chipboard (American Crafts)
Punch (McGill, Inc., Fiskars)
Ribbon (BasicGrey)
Paper trimmer or scissors
Adhesive of choice

Sweet Bird Card

by Vivian Masket

This sweet birdie card is perfect to have in your card stash to use for any occasion.
Add a note of gratitude or thinking of you on the inside and you are set to go.

1 Fold a 10" ×5" (25.5cm × 12.75cm) piece of brown cardstock in half to create a 5" × 5" (12.75cm × 12.75cm) square card base.

2 Cut a 4" × 4¾" (10.25cm × 12cm) piece of pink cardstock and stamp the background image on it. Add the photo corners to the corners of the paper. Adhere the paper to the front of the card.

3 Cut a 2¼" × 4" (5.75cm × 10.25cm) piece of kraft card-stock and adhere it to the front of the card.

4 Cut a 1½" × 4" (3.75cm × 10.25cm) piece of cream cardstock and stamp the script text image on it. Adhere it to the front of the card. Machine stitch along the bottom edge.

5 Cut a 2½" × 2½" (6.25cm × 6.25cm) piece of brown card-stock and adhere it to the front of the card with foam adhesive.

6 Cut a 2¼" × 2¼" (5.75cm × 5.75cm) piece of kraft cardstock and stamp it with a polka dot image, then adhere it to the front of the card. Adhere the felt bird to the front of the card.

SUPPLIES

Cardstock (Core'dinations) • Stamps (Hero Arts) • Felt shape (Martha Stewart Crafts) • Photo corners (3L) • Paper trimmer or scissors • Adhesive of choice • Foam adhesive • Sewing machine

Missing You Birdie Card

by Kimber McGray

The soft rainy image of the birds expresses the thought of missing a friend.
Send this card to a friend to let her know she is missed.

1 Fold a 10" × 7" (25.5cm × 17.75cm) piece of blue patterned paper in half to create a 5" × 7" (12.75cm × 17.75cm) card base.

2 Cut a 6¾" × 4¾" (17cm × 12cm) theme patterned paper and adhere it to the front of the card.

3 Punch a ½" × 4¾" (1.25cm × 12cm) pink piece of cardstock with a border punch. Adhere it to the front edge of the card.

4 Tie a bow in a piece of sheer ribbon, and attach it to the front. Wrap the top end of the ribbon around the back and the bottom end around to the inside of the card, and attach both ends.

5 Embellish the card with gemstones.

SUPPLIES

Cardstock (Bazzill Basics)

Patterned paper (BoBunny Press, Autumn Leaves)

Ribbon (May Arts)

Punch (Stampin' Up!)

Gemstones (Zva Creative)

Paper trimmer or scissors

Adhesive of choice

Sympathy Flowers Card

by Sharon Harnist

The soft coloring of the flowers expresses your condolences to a friend. Sharon shows how to bring a beautiful image out by coloring it with markers.

1 Fold an 8½" × 5½" (21.5cm × 14cm) piece of brown patterned paper in half to create a 4¼" × 5½" (10.75cm × 14cm) card base.

2 Cut a 4¼" × 5½" (10.75cm × 14cm) piece of patterned paper and adhere it to the front of the card base.

3 Cut a 4" × 5¼" (10.25cm × 13.25cm) piece of floral patterned paper and machine stitch it to the front of the card base. Distress the edges.

4 Color a white silk ribbon with a Copic Marker and tie it around the card front.

5 Handcut or die cut a piece of pink patterned paper and color the edges with a Copic Marker that coordinates with the papers. Adhere it to the front of the card.

6 Stamp a floral image and color it in with Copic Markers. Adhere it to front of the card.

SUPPLIES

Cardstock (Taylored Expressions)
Patterned paper (Webster's Pages)
Stamp (Lockhart Stamp Company)
Markers and glitter pen (Copic)
Ink (Tsukineko, Ranger Industries)
Die (Spellbinders)
Ribbon (Creative Impressions)
Paper trimmer or scissors
Adhesive of choice
Sewing machine

See the Copic Marker technique on page 19 to learn how to use these markers.

May Peace Be With You Sympathy Card

by Kimber McGray

The monotone color palette and reflective stamp image is the perfect combination for a sympathy card for a friend or family member.

1 Fold a 10½" × 5¼" (26.5cm × 13.25cm) piece of cream cardstock in half to create a 5¼" × 5¼" (13.25cm × 13.25cm) card base.

2 Tear the bottom edges of the card with a deckled edge tearing ruler.

3 Cut a 5" × 4½" (12.75cm × 11.5cm) piece of patterned paper with a decorative edge.

Layer a tan piece of cardstock behind it and trim around the edge to create a thin tan border. Adhere the paper to the front of the card.

4 Stamp the tree image on the front of the patterned paper.

5 Tie a piece of twine around the front of the card and staple it into place.

SUPPLIES

Cardstock (Core'dinations)

Patterned paper (Making Memories)

Decorative ruler (Fiskars)

Stamp (Inkadinkado)

Ink (VersaColor by Tsukineko)

Twine (Jillibean Soup)

Stapler

Paper trimmer or scissors

Adhesive of choice

Welcome to the Neighborhood Cookie Box

by Kimber McGray

Card making supplies can easily be used to decorate a plain box. Fill it with cookies to welcome your new neighbors.

Supplies:

Gable box (Michaels); patterned paper (Crate Paper); die cuts (Crate Paper); ribbon (Creative Impressions); punch (Stampin' Up!, EK Success)

Butterfly Gift Box

by Lisa Dorsey

Lisa created an elegant way to give a gift of homemade treats, a set of candles or a small gift by dressing up a simple kraft box you can buy at a craft store.

Supplies:

Patterned paper (Anna Griffin); sticker (Anna Griffin); gemstones (Prima Marketing, Inc.); box, ribbon (craft store)

Rose Card
by Barb Albrecht

Flourish Circle Card
by Terry Moore

Supplies:

Cardstock (Die Cuts With a View); patterned paper (Jillibean Soup); stamp (Penny Black, Inc.); metal dots (Colorbök)

Supplies

Cardstock (Bazzill Basics); patterned paper (BasicGrey, BoBunny Press); die cut (QuicKutz); punch (McGill, Inc.); ink (ColorBox by Clearsnap)

Bird on a Branch Card
by Terry Moore

Winged Wishes
by Teza Hampton

Chocolate and Flowers Card
by Teza Hampton

Supplies:

Cardstock (Bazzill Basics); die cut (QuicKutz); punch (EK Success)

Supplies:

Cardstock (Bazzill Basics); patterned paper (My Mind's Eye); flowers (Prima Marketing, Inc.); glitter (Tattered Angels); brad (American Crafts); die cut (Jenni Bowlin Studio); ink (Ranger Industries); embossing folder (Provo Craft Cuttlebug); colored pencils (Prismacolor)

Supplies:

Cardstock (Die Cuts With a View); patterned paper (Die Cuts With a View); flowers (Prima Marketing, Inc.); brad (American Crafts); punch (Fiskars); ribbon (May Arts); twine (May Arts)

Pink and Brown Flower Card
by Sherry Wright

Thinking of You Flower Card
by Pat Sergeant

Owl In Window Card
by Nathalie Leonelli

Supplies:

Cardstock (Prism Papers); patterned paper (BoBunny Press); ink (Clearsnap)

Supplies:

Cardstock (Bazzill Basics); patterned paper (Stampin' Up!); gemstones (Recollections); ribbon (Michaels); embossing folder (Provo Craft Cuttlebug)

Supplies:

Cardstock (Bazzill Basics, DMD by Creativity Inc.); patterned paper (Nikki Sivils Scrapbooker); ribbon (American Crafts); transparency (office supply store); brad

Missing You Balloon Card
by Terri Hayes

Hello, Sunshine Card
by Andrea Amu

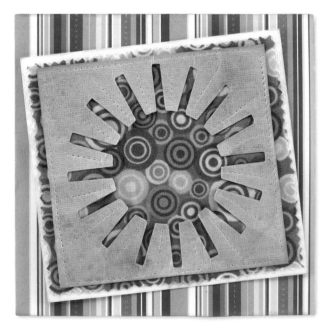

Supplies:

Cardstock (Bazzill Basics); patterned paper (Webster's Pages); die cuts (Making Memories); vintage trim

Supplies:

Cardstock (Bazzill Basics); patterned paper (Tinkering Ink); ink (Clearsnap, Tattered Angels); die cuts (Provo Craft Cricut)

Cheery Cherry Note Card
by Sharon Harnist

Red Kraft Butterfly Card
by Ellen Sosnoski

Owl Card
by Ellen Sosnoski

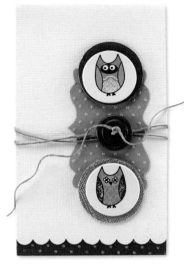

Supplies:

Cardstock (Neenah, Papertrey Ink); note cards (The Paper Studio); stamps (Lockhart Stamp Company); markers (Copic); ink (Tsukineko); dies (Spellbinders); ribbon (Michaels)

Supplies:

Cardstock (Core'dinations); patterned paper (Jillibean Soup); button (Jillibean Soup); twine (Jillibean Soup); die cut (Jillibean Soup)

Supplies:

Cardstock (Core'dinations and Bazzill Basics); chipboard (Prima Marketing, Inc.); buttons (Autumn Leaves by Creativity Inc.); die cut (Creative Cuts and More); embossing folder (Provo Craft Cuttlebug); punches (Creative Memories, Stampin' Up!)

Happy Bird Card
by Debbie Standard

Butterfly Card
by Jenn Biederman

Supplies:

Cardstock (Core'dinations); patterned paper (Best Creation, Inc.); gemstones (Reminisce)

Supplies:

Cardstock (DMD by Creativity Inc.); patterned paper (BasicGrey); stamps (Purple Onion Designs); ink (Ranger Industries, Top Boss by Clearsnap); embossing powder (American Crafts); ribbon (Really Reasonable Ribbon); gemstones (Hero Arts)

Sunflower Card
by Melissa Phillips

Butterfly Friendship Card
by Lynn Ghahary

Colorful Flower Card
by Lynn Ghahary

Supplies:

Cardstock (Papertrey Ink); patterned paper (Jillibean Soup); die cut (Jillibean Soup); ribbon (Jillibean Soup); sticker (Jenni Bowlin Studio); button (Hero Arts); gemstones (Zva Creative); stamps (Papertrey Ink); ink (Papertrey Ink)

Supplies:

Cardstock (Bazzill Basics); patterned paper (Pebbles Inc.); buttons (Sassafras Lass); stickers (Pebbles Inc.); punch (EK Success)

Supplies:

Cardstock (Bazzill Basics); patterned paper (KI Memories); ribbon (Michaels); flowers (Prima Marketing, Inc.); gemstones (BasicGrey); die cuts (KI Memories); stickers (KI Memories); punches (EK Success)

Friendship Flower Card
by Laura Vegas

New House Card
by Kelly Goree

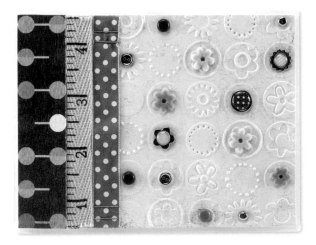

Supplies:

Cardstock (BasicGrey); patterned paper (My Mind's Eye); ribbon (Jillibean Soup); brads (Making Memories); embossing folder (Provo Craft Cuttlebug); staples

Supplies:

Cardstock (Bazzill Basics); patterned paper (BasicGrey); chipboard (BasicGrey); punches (Fiskars)

Patchwork Bird Card
by Stacey Kingman

Supplies:

Cardstock (Prism Papers); die cut (Jenni Bowlin Studio); ink (Ranger Industries, Palette by Stewart Superior); patterned paper (October Afternoon); gemstones (K&Company); stamp (October Afternoon)

Flowers in a Vase Card
by Tami Mayberry

Supplies:

Cardstock (Prism Papers); patterned paper (Jillibean Soup); vellum (Prism Papers); stamp (Gina K Designs); die cut (Spellbinders); gemstones (Kaisercraft); ribbon (Creative Impressions); markers (Copic); ink (Clearsnap)

Berry Card
by Tami Mayberry

Supplies:

Cardstock (Prism Papers); patterned paper (Sassafras Lass); dies (Spellbinders); felt embellishment (Sassafras Lass); gemstones (Creative Impressions)

Have a Seat Friendship or New Home Card
by Kristie Larsen

Supplies:

Cardstock (Papertrey Ink); patterned postcard print (Hambly); vintage buttons (Papertrey Ink); Twine (Papertrey Ink); pen (Gelly Roll)

Strawberries on a Windowsill
by Tina Fussell

Supplies:

Cardstock (Papertrey Ink); patterned paper (Stampin' Up!); twine

Button Flower Card
by Kristie Larsen

Supplies:

Cardstock (Papertrey Ink); patterned paper (Papertrey Ink); buttons (Papertrey ink); stamps (Papertrey Ink); ink (Stampin' Up!); ribbon (American Crafts); punch (EK Success)

Card Sketches

Use these card sketches as templates to re-create cards or as guidance for proportions and embellishment placement.

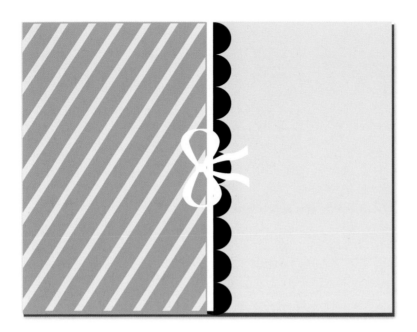

Completed card on page 89.

Completed card on page 41.

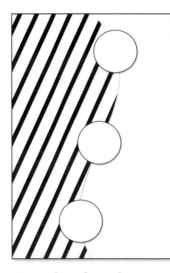

Completed card on page 106.

Completed card on page 67.

Completed card on page 70.

Completed card on page 81.

Completed card on page 98.

Completed card on page 41.

Completed card on page 99.

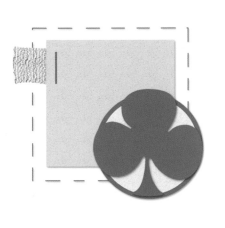

Completed card on page 80.

Sample Sentiments

Birthday

Happy Birthday

Happy Sweet 16

May Your Birthday Be Filled
With Beautiful Things

Hoping You Have a
Sweet Birthday

Happy Birthday to
Someone Sweet

Beep! Beep! That's "Happy
Birthday" in Robot!

Happy Birthday Human!

Happy Birthday to
My Favorite Boy

Have an Awesome Birthday

Baby's 1st Birthday

The Big 4-0

Christmas/Winter Holidays

Merry Christmas

Home for the Holidays

From Our House to Yours

Wishing You a Merry
Little Christmas

Season's Greetings!

Glad Tidings to You This
Holiday Season

Blessings at Christmas

Happy Holidays

Warm Wishes

Let It Snow

Snowflake Dreams

Glad Tidings

Oh, Christmas Tree

Hanukkah Holiday Wishes

Other Holidays

Valentines' Day

To the One I Love

You Make My Heart Sing

You Have My Heart

Happy Valentine's Day
to My One and Only

All My Love

Love Has Wings

Halloween

Have a Spooktacular
Halloween

Boo!

Go Batty

Mother's Day

Happy Mother's Day

Thank You, Mom, for
All That You Do!

Father's Day

Happy Father's Day

Super Dad!

You're TEE-riffic, Dad!

Thanksgiving

Give Thanks

So Thankful

Special Day

Wedding

So Happy for You

Let Your Dreams Take Flight

Always and Forever

On Your Special Day

For the Bride and Groom

Anniversary

We Make Quite a "Pear"

It's apPEARent We Were
Meant To Be Together

Baby

Welcome Little One!

Congratulations on Your
Newest Addition!

Graduation

Congrats Grad!

Way to Go!

Shoot for the Stars!

Sweet Sentiments

New Home

Congratulations on
Your New Home

We've Moved

Bloom Where You Are Planted

Thinking of You

For My Wonderful Friend!

Thank You for Your Friendship

Hello, Friend

For My Sweet Daughter

Hey, Sunshine!

If Friends Were Flowers,
I'd Pick You

Resources

The following companies manufacture products featured in this book. Please check your local retailers to find these materials, or go to a company's Web site for the latest product. In addition, we have made every attempt to properly credit the items mentioned in this book. We apologize to any company that we have listed incorrectly, and we would appreciate hearing from you.

3L Corporation—Scrapbook Adhesives
www.scrapbook-adhesives.com

3M
www.3m.com

American Crafts
www.americancrafts.com

Anna Griffin, Inc.
www.annagriffin.com

ANW Crestwood
www.anwcrestwood.com

Archiver's
www.archiversonline.com

Autumn Leaves
www.autumnleaves.com

BasicGrey
www.basicgrey.com

Bazzill Basics Paper
www.bazzillbasics.com

Bella Blvd
www.bellablvd.net

Berwick Offray, LLC
www.offray.com

Best Creation, Inc.
www.bestcreation.us

BoBunny Press
www.bobunny.com

Clearsnap, Inc.
www.clearsnap.com

Close To My Heart
www.closetomyheart.com

Colorbök, Inc.
www.colorbok.com

Copic Markers
www.copicmarker.com

Core'dinations
www.coredinations.com

Cornish Heritage Farms
www.cornishheritagefarms.com

Cosmo Cricket
www.cosmocricket.com

Crate Paper, Inc.
www.cratepaper.com

Creative Cuts and More
www.creativecutsandmore.com

Creative Imaginations
www.cigift.com

Creative Impressions
www.creativeimpressions.com

Creative Memories
www.creativememories.com

Creativity Inc.
www.creativityinc.com

Cutter Bee—see EK Success, Ltd.

Deja Views
www.dejaviews.com

Denami Design Rubber Stamps
www.denamidesign.com

Die Cuts With A View
www.diecutswithaview.com

DMC Corp.
www.dmc-usa.com

DMD Paper—see Creativity, Inc.

Doodlebug Design, Inc.
www.doodlebug.ws

Dream Street Papers
www.dreamstreetpapers.com

EK Success, Ltd.
www.eksuccess.com

Expo International, Inc.
www.expointl.com

Fancy Pants Designs, LLC
www.fancypantsdesigns.com

Fiskars, Inc.
www.fiskars.com

Flower Soft
www.flower-soft.com

GCD Studios
www.gcdstudios.com

Georgia-Pacific Corporation
www.gp.com

Gina K Designs
www.ginakdesigns.ning.com

Glitz Design, LLC
www.glitzitnow.com

Graphic 45
www.g45papers.com

Hambly Studios/Hambly Screenprints
www.hamblyscreenprints.com

Hanna Stamps
www.hannastamps.com

Heidi Swapp/Advantus Corporation
www.heidiswapp.com

Hero Arts Rubber Stamps, Inc.
www.heroarts.com

Imaginisce
www.imaginisce.com

Impression Obsession, Inc.
www.impression-obsession.com

Inchie Arts, LLC
www.inchiearts.com

Jenni Bowlin
www.jennibowlin.com

Jesse James & Co., Inc.
www.jessejamesbutton.com

Jillibean Soup
www.jillibean-soup.com

Jo-Ann Stores
www.joann.com

Jolee's Boutique—see EK Success, Ltd.

K&Company
www.kandcompany.com

Kaisercraft
www.kaisercraft.net

KI Memories, Inc,
www.kimemories.com

Krylon
www.krylon.com

Li'l Davis Designs
www.lildavisdesigns.typepad.com

Lockhart Stamp Company, LLC
www.lockhartstampcompany.com

Luxe Designs
www.luxedesigns.com

Making Memories
www.makingmemories.com

Marcella by K—see K&Company

Martha Stewart Crafts
www.marthastewartcrafts.com

Resources

Marvy Uchida/ Uchida of America, Corp.
www.uchida.com

Maya Road, LLC
www.mayaroad.com

May Arts
www.mayarts.com

McGill, Inc.
www.mcgillinc.com

me & my BIG ideas
www.meandmybigideas.com

Melissa Frances/Heart & Home, Inc.
www.melissafrances.com

Michaels Arts & Crafts
www.michaels.com

Microsoft Corporation
www.microsoft.com

Mohawk Paper Mills, Inc.
www.mohawkpaperstore.com

MultiCrafts & Gifts, Inc.
www.multicrafts.com

My Mind's Eye, Inc.
www.mymindseye.com

Neenah Paper, Inc.
www.neenahpaper.com

Nikki Sivilis, Scrapbooker
www.nikkisivils.com

October Afternoon
www.octoberafternoon.com

Paperbilities—see Westrim, Inc.

Paper Company, The—see ANW Crestwood

Paper Reflections—see DMD Industries

Paper Studio, The
www.paperstudio.com

Papertrey Ink
www.papertreyink.com

Pebbles Inc.
www.pebblesinc.com

Penny Black, Inc.
www.pennyblackinc.com

Piggy Tales
www.piggytales.com

Pink Paislee
www.pinkpaislee.com

Pink Persimmon
www.pinkpersimmon.com

Prima Marketing, Inc.
www.primamarketinginc.com

Prismacolor by Sanford
www.prismacolor.com

Provo Craft
www.provocraft.com

Purple Onion Designs
www.purpleoniondesigns.com

Queen & Co.
www.queenandcompany.com

QuicKutz, Inc.
www.quickutz.com

Ranger Industries, Inc.
www.rangerink.com

Really Reasonable Ribbon
www.reasonableribbon.com

Reminisce Papers
www.shopreminisce.com

Riff Raff Designs
riffraffdesigns.typepad.com

Sandylion Sticker Designs
www.sandylion.com

Sanford Corporation
www.sanfordcorp.com

Sassafras Lass
www.sassafraslass.com

Scenic Route Paper Co.
www.scenicroutepaper.com

Scor-Pal
www.scor-pal.com

Scotch tape—see 3M

SEI, Inc.
www.shopsei.com

Sharpie—see Sanford

Sharon Ann Collection—see Deja Views

Sizzix
www.sizzix.com

Spellbinders Paper Arts, LLC
www.spellbinders.us

Stampabilities/Crafts, Etc!
www.stampabilities.com

Stampin' Up!
www.stampinup.com

Stewart Superior Corporation
www.stewartsuperior.com

Studio Calico
www.studiocalico.com

Tattered Angels
www.mytatteredangels.com

Taylored Expressions
www.tayloredexpressions.com

Technique Tuesday, LLC
www.techniquetuesday.com

Tinkering Ink
www.tinkeringink.com

Top Boss—see Clearsnap

Tsukineko, LLC
www.tsukineko.com

Uni-ball/Sanford
www.uniball-na.com

Unity Stamp Company
www.unitystampco.com

Wal-Mart Stores, Inc.
www.walmart.com

Wausau Papers
www.wausaupaper.com

Webster's Pages/Webster Fine Art Limited
www.websterspages.com

We R Memory Keepers
www.weronthenet.com

Westrim Crafts
www.creativityinc.com

Wrights Ribbon Accents
www.wrights.com

Zing Embossing Powder—see American Crafts

Zva Creative
www.zvacreative.com

Index

Get more paper inspiration!

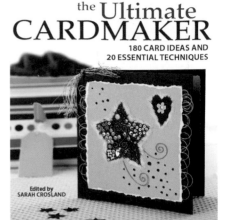

Girlfriend Greetings

Edited by Christine Doyle

Inside you'll find sixty simple and sassy cards to give to your friends for every occasion, including celebratory greetings for birthdays and new jobs, and even consolation cards for nasty breakups and bad haircuts. In addition to the fabulous cards, you'll also get cheeky sidebars and technique tips.

ISBN-10: 1-58180-862-3
ISBN-13: 978-1-58180-862-9
paperback, 96 pages, Z0274

Simply Cards

By Sally Traidman

From birthdays to holidays and for all occasions in between, turn to the bright and breezy style of the cards featured in Simply Cards. The candy colors, spring brights and retro hues of these cards give them a fresh and playful look that's sure to appeal to anyone who receives one of these simple and graphic missives. You'll get maximum yield for minimum time with the cards in this book.

ISBN-10: 1-58180-674-4
ISBN-13: 978-1-58180-674-8
paperback, 128 pages, 33260

The Ultimate Card Maker

From the editors of Crafts Beautiful Magazine

From beading, wire work, and die-cuts, to stitcing, polymer clay, and quilling, this guide provides innovative ways to craft amazing and quick-to-make greeting cards. With twenty featured techniques and eight additional card inspirations per project, you will never be at a loss when trying to find that perfect greeting!

ISBN 10: 0-7153-2596-5
ISBN 13: 978-0-7153-2596-4
paprback, 256 pages, Z0877

These and other fine F+W Media titles are available at your local craft retailer, bookstore or online supplier, or visit our Web site at www.mycraftivitystore.com.

An online place for paper people

Find up-to-date trends, news, reviews, inspiration and ideas at
www.memorymakersmagazine.com.